Annapurna

...an offering of Indian recipes

Uma Shetty

toExcel

San Jose New York Lincoln Shanghai

Annapurna
...an offering of Indian recipes

Published by toExcel
an imprint of iUniverse.com, Inc.

For information address:
iUniverse.com, Inc.
620 North 48th Street
Suite 201
Lincoln, NE 68504-3467
www.iuniverse.com

ISBN: 0-595-00123-8

Printed in the United States of America

"Annapurna"
(Goddess of plenty)

Goddess Parvathi dwells in yet another form on the sacred mountain peaks of the Himalayas known as Annapurna, named after her.

Annapurna in Sanskrit means "She who is filled with food." Annapurna is regarded as a purely benevolent deity, a kindhearted Goddess of plenty. She is the queen of Benaras, the holy city of the Hindus on the banks of the Ganges, south of Nepal. Each year, after the autumn harvest, the people of Benaras celebrate a festival dedicated to Her called Annakuta, "the food Mountain," in which they fill her temple with a mountain of food — rice, lentils, and sweets of all kinds to be distributed to whose who come to receive Her blessings.

Table of Contents

BREAKFAST DISHES

RICE DISHES

VEGETARIAN CURRIES

NON VEGETARIAN DISHES

SNACKS AND SWEETS

CAKES AND BISCUITS

DESSERTS

INGREDIENTS

Forward

Mrs. Uma Shetty's home has always been a Gourmet's Paradise, whenever we, the people of Bellary have been invited. For several years, the ladies especially have wanted to know the recipes of the wonderful tasty fare she has always served her guests — whether it was breakfast, lunch, tea or dinner. She has always been very innovative and has used the variety of fruits and vegetables from her garden. She not only makes the food tasty, but garnishes the various dishes so attractively that her table looks beautifully set on every occasion.

I cannot thank her enough for responding to our request to share her recipes with us. "Uma Aunty" or "Uma Akka" as she is affectionately known among her friends and relatives has achieved this culinary art with minimum help but maximum largesse of heart.

I am sure you will enjoy possessing and using this cook book and wish you "bon appetite"!

Dr. Alice Doraiswamy

*This book is dedicated to Uma Shetty by her family
as a loving tribute to her culinary artistry.*

Acknowledgement

*Special thanks to Krupa, who compiled the recipes
and made this book a reality.*

For questions and inquiries regarding recipes or to obtain ingredients,
send e-mail to vinishetty@aol.com.

Proceeds from the sale of this book will be donated to
Bunts Association of Bellary
(A community charitable organization in India.)

Soups, Salads and Raithas

CREAM OF TOMATO SOUP

6 large tomatoes, chopped
1 large onion, chopped
1 stick, celery chopped
5 cups water
 2 small carrots, chopped

2 tbs. all purpose flour
2 tbs. butter
1/3 cup milk
Salt and pepper to taste

Pressure cook tomatoes, onion, celery, and carrots with water.
Pass through a sieve. Melt butter. Add the flour and stir well.
Add the pureed mixture along with milk and boil for a few
minutes. Serve hot with cream and croutons.

CREAM OF SPINACH SOUP

450 grams (1 lb.) spinach
1 onion finely chopped
1 onion cubed
1 tbs. butter

2 tbs. flour
4 cups milk
Salt and pepper to taste

Boil spinach and cubed onion with a little water. Puree it. Sauté
the chopped onion in butter. Add flour and mix well. Next, add salt,
pepper, and milk to it, mix well and cook for a few minutes. Add
the spinach puree and cook for five minutes. Serve hot with cream.

VEGETABLE CORN SOUP

1 16 oz. can of cream style corn
2 med. carrots, chopped
1 1/2 cups cabbage, chopped
1 onion, sliced
10 green beans chopped

2 tbs. butter
1 cup milk
1 cup water
Salt to taste
1 tbsp. dissolved corn flour
   (optional)

Boil the corn in a pot, adding enough water to cover, and cook
on a low flame. Sauté the carrots and beans in one tbs. butter
till half-done. Add this to the corn with salt. Heat the remain-

ing butter and sauté the onions till tender. To this, add cabbage and cook for a few minutes, add water and milk and let it boil. Cool the cabbage and blend to a puree. Add this to the corn with the corn flour and boil for five minutes. Serve hot with cream.

CHICKEN CORN SOUP

1 16 oz. can cream style corn	2 eggs
6 cups water	Salt and pepper to taste
2 tbs. corn flour	2 chicken bullion cubes
1 cup boiled and shredded chicken	

Boil the corn in six cups water till tender. Add corn flour mixed in a little flour. Add boiled and shredded chicken, the chicken bullion cubes, salt, and pepper. Let it boil. Lastly, pour beaten egg and stir slowly with a fork, till it thickens. Serve hot with chili sauce. To make chili sauce:

Chili Sauce:	2 tbs. vinegar
Chopped green chilies	1/2 tbs. soy sauce
1 cup water	Salt to taste

Mix all ingredients and serve with soup.

CARROT SOUP

2 large carrots, cubed	2 1/4 cups milk
1 tbs. butter	1 tbs. heavy cream
1 tsp. pepper corns	Salt to taste
1 tbs. corn flour	

Heat the butter. Add pepper corns till it crackles. Add corn flour and stir a little. Immediately add chopped carrots and fry a little. Add milk and boil. Cool and blend in a blender. Boil this mixture once more. Add salt to taste. Garnish with heavy cream and serve.

APPLE SOUP

225 gms. (1/2 lb.) apples,
 peeled and chopped
1/2 cup milk
1/2 cup carrots grated
2 tbs. sugar
1/2 tbs. lemon juice

a few sprigs of mint leaves
a large pinch of cinnamon
2 tbs. butter
1 tbs. corn flour
Salt to taste

Melt butter, add chopped apples and sugar and stir a little. Add six cups water. Cover and cook for 10 minutes till the apple pieces are soft. Cool and puree the mixture. To this add the grated carrots, and the flour dissolved in milk. Add lemon juice, cinnamon powder, and salt to taste. Cook for five minutes and serve hot, garnished with mint leaves.

CHINESE NOODLE SOUP

100 gms. noodles
6 cups vegetable stock
1/2 cup chopped spring onion
1/2 tsp. garlic paste
1/2 tsp. ginger paste
1 tbs. corn flour
Salt to taste

1 tsp. oil
1 tbs. soy sauce
1/2 tsp. pepper
a pinch of ajinomoto
 (optional)
1 tsp. sherry or wine

Heat oil in a wok. Add ginger and garlic paste and fry for a minute. Add vegetable stock and cook for five minutes. Dissolve corn flour in 2 tbs. water and add to the soup mixture. Add soy sauce and sherry. Boil noodles in salted water separately. Drain and place them in individual bowls. Pour the prepared stock on noodles. Top with chopped spring onions. Serve hot with Chili sauce.

GREEN PEAS SOUP

1/4 kg. green peas
2 onions, chopped
2 cups white sauce
  (recipe on pg. 18)

6 tbs. fresh cream
1 cup croutons
Salt and pepper to taste

Boil peas and onions in 4 cups water. Blend and strain. Return to pot. Add white sauce, salt and pepper and mix thoroughly. Serve hot garnished with fresh cream and croutons.

COLESLAW

4 cups cabbage (sliced thinly)
2 capsicum (sliced thinly)
1 onion (sliced thinly)
500 gms. pineapple
  (drained well and diced)

1 cup grated cheese
1/2 cup mayonnaise
2 tbs. lemon juice
1/2 cup whipped cream

Mix together all vegetables. Add mayonnaise, lemon juice, cheese, and whipped cream. Toss well. Refrigerate until chilled.

TRICOLOR SALAD RING

200 gms. grated carrots
250 gms. cooked rice
2 cups mayonnaise

250 gms. capsicum
  (finely chopped)

METHOD Lightly spray a jelly mcld or a bundt cake pan. Mix the grated carrots with mayonnaise and layer the dish. Press firmly. Next, layer the rice and press firmly. Lastly, layer the capsicum pressing firmly. Cover and chill for sometime. Unmould it on a bed of lettuce before serving.

MACARONI SALAD

1/2 cup onion (finely chopped)
2 cups macaroni
2 tbs. salt
2 tbs. ajwain (carom seeds)
1 tsp. chili powder
1 tsp. mustard
1 pod garlic (finely chopped)

2 cups macaroni 1/2 cup sugar
(boiled and drained)
2 big carrots (grated)
1 onion (finely chopped)
2 cups croutons
2 potatoes (boiled and cubed)

Mix the chopped onions, sugar, salt, ajwain, chili powder, mustard, and garlic in a blender to form a thick sauce. Add this sauce to the boiled macaroni and potato cubes. Toss well. Refrigerate until chilled. Garnish with croutons and grated carrots just before serving.

RUSSIAN SALAD

2 carrots (finely chopped)
200 gms. cabbage shredded
1 cup boiled peas
3 potatoes boiled and cubed
2 capsicum (finely chopped)
3 ring slices of pineapple (finely chopped)

100 gms. seedless grapes
25 gms. walnuts, chopped
1 large apple, diced
2 cups mayonnaise

Mix all the ingredients in a bowl. Refrigerate until chilled.

CRISP CARROT MOULD

1 cup mayonnaise
1/4 cup cream cheese
1 1/2 cups pineapple pieces
1 1/2 cups carrots (grated)
1/2 cup whipped cream

2 cups orange juice
2 tbs. gelatin
1/2 tsp. mustard powder
1 tsp. pepper powder
Salt to taste

Dissolve the gelatin in orange juice in a double boiler. Set it in the fridge. Remove and add mayonnaise, cream cheese, pineapple pieces, and the rest of the ingredients and toss well. Pour this mixture into a lightly greases salad bowl. Refrigerate until set. Unmould and serve on a bed of grated cabbage and mint leaves.

CRUNCHY CUCUMBER AND BANANA SALAD

2 medium sized cucumbers

2 ripe bananas

2 onions

1 bunch coriander leaves, chopped

1/2 tsp. pepper

2 cups yogurt or curd

Salt to taste

Cut the cucumber into four parts lengthwise and slice finely. Cut the bananas in half and slice. Chop onions. Mix well with yogurt. Add salt or pepper to taste. Garnish with coriander leaves. Chill and serve.

APPLE AND YOGURT SALAD

2 apples

2 cups yogurt (curd)

1 cup freshly grated coconut

2 tbs. sugar

Salt to taste

1/2 tsp. Pepper

1 tbs. coriander leaves
  (finely chopped)

1 green chili (finely chopped)

Seasoning

1/2 tsp. cumin seeds

1/2 tsp. mustard seeds

1/2 tsp. urad dal
  (skinless split black beans)

2 dry red chilies

1 sprig curry leaves

1 tbs. oil

Core and peel the apples and chop into fine pieces. Mix this with the grated coconut and yogurt. Add salt, sugar, and pepper to taste. Add chilies and chopped coriander. Heat oil, add the mustard and cumin seeds till they crackle. Add urad dal and brown. Add curry leaves and red chilies. Garnish the salad with this seasoning. Serve chilled.

TRIFLE SALAD

1/2 apple diced
1/2 banana diced
3 rings pineapple diced
2 tbs. walnuts
1 tbs. raisins
boiled potatoes diced
boiled peas 50 gms.
boiled and chopped French beans

Dressing
1/2 cup pineapple juice
1 tsp. salad oil
2 tsp. rum (optional)
50 gms. cream 100 gms.
Salt to taste 50 gms.

Mix all the dressing ingredients in a blender and chill. Mix all the fruits and vegetables in a large salad bowl and toss. Add the dressing and toss well. Chill and serve.

CAULIFLOWER SALAD

1 small sized cauliflower
3 tbs. vinegar or lime juice
1 tsp. sugar
2 cups water
2 tbs. oil

1/2 tsp. mustard seeds
a pinch of nutmeg powder
1 tbs. fresh coriander chopped
1/2 tsp. chopped ginger
Salt to taste

Break cauliflower into flowerets and cook in rapid boiling water with sugar and salt. Remove when just done and not too soft and strain. Arrange in a flat dish. Heat oil and add mustard seeds. Remove as they crackle. Add ginger salt and nutmeg powder. Mix well and pour over cauliflower. Chill and serve garnished with fresh coriander.

TROPICAL SALAD

1 cup paneer (cream cheese)
(cut into small cubes)
1/3 cup thick yogurt or curd
(beaten)
2 slices pineapple
(cut into small cubes)
1/2 cup tender coconut (sliced finely)
1/4 tsp. pepper
Salt to taste

Pineapple Sauce
1 tsp. butter
1 tsp. cornflour
1 cup pineapple juice
(concentrate)

Soak paneer cubes in salted hot water for five minutes. Drain. Dissolve cornflour in the pineapple juice to form a smooth paste. Melt butter in a pan. Add the cornflour paste to the pan and cook, stirring well to avoid lumps. Remove and cool. To this, add yogurt, salt and pepper powder. Finally, add the pineapple cubes and tender coconut to the sauce. Refrigerate and serve.

CABBAGE SALAD

1 medium sized cabbage
1 cup thin noodles
6 spring onions
15 almonds
2 tbs. sesame seeds
2 tbs. sesame seeds

Dressing
1 1/2 tbs. oil
7 tbs. vinegar
7 tbs. powdered sugar
1 1/2 tsp. pepper
Salt to taste

METHOD Mix all the dressing ingredients in a bottle. Shake well and refrigerate to thicken. Cut cabbage into 2" cubes, and place in ice-cold water for ten minutes. Heat a tsp. of oil and fry the noodles lightly. Set aside. Blanch almonds and slice thinly and toast in a tsp. of oil, till it crackles. Mix the cabbage with the dressing. Garnish with sesame seeds, noodles, chopped spring onions, and toasted almonds.

BREAD CROUTONS AND SPROUT SALAD

Crouton Layer
4 slices of bread
oil for deep frying
chili powder
salt to taste

Mint Sauce
2 sprigs mint leaves
2 sprigs coriander leaves
2 green chilies
1/2 tsp. cumin powder
1/4 tsp. salt
1/2 cup fresh yogurt or curd
  (beaten)

Sprout Layer
1/2 cup sprouted moong dal
1/2 cup sprouted channa dal
1 tbs. oil
salt to taste

Topping
1 cup fresh yogurt or curd
  (beaten)
1 tbs. chaat masala powder
15 gms. chopped corriander

Cut bread into half inch cubes and deep fry in hot oil till golden brown. Sprinkle salt and chili powder and set aside. Heat 1 tbs. oil in a pan. Fry the sprouted dals. Add salt to taste and set aside. For the mint sauce, grind all the ingredients except yogurt to a paste. Add yogurt and mix. Put the masala bread croutons in a deep dish. Cover with mint sauce. Next layer it with bean sprouts. Finally, top with fresh beaten yogurt. Sprinkle chaat masala, garnish with chopped coriander leaves and serve immediately.

BANANA RAITHA

1 cup yogurt
3 bananas sliced
1 cup grated coconut
2 green chilies

1/4 tsp. mustard seeds
1 tsp. chopped coriander
  leaves
1 tsp. oil
salt to taste

Lightly beat yogurt. To this add chopped bananas, grated coconut, coriander, and salt to taste. Heat oil. Add mustard seeds, green chilies, and curry leaves. Pour this seasoning over the yogurt mixture. Mix and serve.

KING SALAD RIATHA

1 small cucumber (cubed)	1 tbs. sugar
4 ripe bananas (cubed)	1/2 tsp. pepper
1 cup yogurt	1 onion, chopped

Mix all ingredients. Chill and serve.

EGGPLANT (Brinjal) RAITHA

1 cup yogurt	1/2 tsp. mustard seeds
1 large eggplant	1 tsp. oil
1 onion	2 tbs. coriander leaves,
2 flakes garlic	chopped
2 green chilies	Salt to taste

Roast, grill, or bake the eggplant till tender. Peel skin and mash. Mix the eggplant with lightly beaten yogurt, coriander leaves, and salt. Heat the oil and fry the mustard seeds. Add chopped onion, chopped garlic, and chopped green chilies. Fry till brown and pour over eggplant. Mix well and serve.

OKRA (Bhendi) RAITHA

1/4 kg or 1/2 lb. okra	1/2 tsp. pepper powder
2 cups yogurt	2 tbs. fresh coriander chopped
1 tsp. chili powder	Salt and sugar to taste
1 tsp. roasted sesame powder	

Slit the okra lengthwise, chop finely and deep fry. Set aside. Mix yogurt, salt, sugar, chili powder, sesame powder, and pepper. Just before serving, add the fried okra and garnish with chopped coriander.

RADISH RAITHA

2 radish, grated
1 sliced onion
4 green Chilies
  (chopped finely)
1/4 tsp. cumin seeds
1/4 tsp. mustard seeds
1 cup yogurt

2 tsp. oil
a sprig of curry leaves
2 tbs. coriander leaves
  chopped
a pinch of asafoetida powder
  (hing)
salt to taste

Grate the radish and squeeze out the juice. Heat oil, add asafoetida, cumin and mustard seeds. When they crackle, add green Chilies, and curry leaves. When brown, remove from heat, add onions, coriander, and the grated radish. Mix with lightly beaten yogurt. Add salt to taste. Mix well and serve.

Chutneys and Sauces

RIPE MANGO SASMI

1 big ripe mango
3 tbs. grated coconut
1/2 tsp. mustard seeds

1 tbs. sugar or jaggery
4 red chilies
salt to taste

Remove the pulp from the mango. Roast the mustard seeds, and red chilies. Add the coconut, sugar, and salt. Grind to a paste. Add this to the mango pulp and mix well.

TOMATO AND ONION CHUTNEY

3-4 tomatoes
3 onions
10 green chilies
1/2 bunch coriander leaves
6 pods garlic

1 cup fresh grated coconut
1 tsp. tamarind
1/4 cup oil
salt to taste

Heat oil. Fry onions, tomatoes, garlic, chilies, tamarind, and coriander leaves till tender. Add coconut and salt and grind to a fine paste.

RED CAPSICUM CHUTNEY

4 red capsicum
4 onions, chopped
6 flakes of garlic
1 tsp. fenugreek seeds (methi)

1 marble sized ball of tamarind
jaggery to taste
1/2 cup oil
salt to taste

Heat oil. Fry all the chopped ingredients till brown and soft. Add jaggery, salt, and tamarind, and grind to a fine paste without adding water. This can be stored for a week.

EGGPLANT (Brinjal) CHUTNEY

2 medium eggplants, chopped
1 cup fresh grated coconut
1/2 lemon sized tamarind
8 green chilies

3 tbs. oil
1/4 tsp. mustard seeds
salt to taste

Heat oil, add mustard seeds and fry till they crackle. Add green chilies, and eggplant and fry well. Add tamarind, coconut, and salt and grind to a paste.

COCONUT CHUTNEY

2 cups grated coconuts
6 green chilies
1 small onion
3 cloves garlic

1/2 lemon size tamarind
1 tbs. oil
salt to taste

Heat oil. Fry onions, chilies, and garlic till brown and soft. Add grated coconut, tamarind, salt to taste, and grind to a fine paste.

RIDGE GOURD (Peerai) CHUTNEY

1 cup thick scrapings
  of ridge gourd
4 tbs. fresh coconut, grated
1 tbs. urad dal
1 tbs. channa dal

6 red chilies, roasted
1/2 lemon size tamarind
4 tbs. oil
salt to taste

Heat oil. Roast both the dals, mustard seeds, and red chilies. Add the ridge gourd scrapings to it and fry together till you get a good aroma. Add grated coconut, and salt and grind to a paste.

MINT (Pudina) CHUTNEY

1 cup fresh mint leaves
1 cup fresh coriander leaves
1/2 lemon sized tamarind

6-8 green chilies
salt and sugar to taste

Grind all the ingredients to a fine paste. Tastes good with snacks.

TOMATO RELISH

12 large tomatoes
4 onions
1 tbs. mustard powder
6-12 green chilies
1 tbs. curry powder (madras)

1 tbs. flour
1 tbs. salt
400 gms. or 1 1/2 cup
   brown sugar
1/4 cup malt vinegar

Skin and slice tomatoes and onions. Layer in a glass bowl, sprinkle with salt and leave overnight. The next day, drain well and boil in a sauce pan with sugar, and chilies for one hour. Add mustard powder, curry powder, flour, and vinegar and boil for ten more minutes. Cool and bottle in sterilized jars. Note: Add more sugar or vinegar according to taste during the last ten minutes of cooking.

MAYONNAISE

2 eggs
1 tsp. mustard powder
1 tsp. pepper
2 tsp. sugar

2 tbs. vinegar
a pinch of salt
1 cup refined oil

Break the eggs and pour into a blender. Add all the remaining ingredients except oil and whip. To this slowly pour the oil till it mixes evenly and the mixture thickens. Remove and pour into jar and store in refrigerator. Can be stored for up to a month.

HOT CHOCOLATE SAUCE

2 tbs. sugar
2 tbs. drinking chocolate
1 tsp. cocoa powder
1/4 tsp. instant coffee powder

a pinch of salt
1 tbs. butter
1 tbs. cornflour
2 cups milk

Boil the milk and add all the remaining ingredients. Cook over double boiler until it thickens. Use as required.

WHITE SAUCE

2 tbs. butter
2 tbs. all-purpose flour

2 cups milk
salt and pepper to taste

Melt the butter. Add flour and cook for one minute, stirring constantly. Remove from heat and gradually add milk. Mix until well combined. Return to heat and cook on low heat stirring continuously until the sauce thickens. Remove, and then add salt and pepper. Mix well.

BARBEQUE SAUCE

2 large tomatoes
1 tbs. brown sugar
1 tbs. soy sauce

2 tsp. vinegar
2 tsp. tomato ketchup
salt to taste

Immerse tomatoes in hot water for ten minutes. Remove skin and chop. Add brown sugar, soy sauce, vinegar, ketchup, and salt and cook for 15 minutes. Use this as a dipping sauce or as marinade for grilling poultry and meat.

CHEESE SAUCE

1 tbs. butter
25 gms. or 1 tbs. grated cheese
200 ml. (about 1 cup) milk

Seasoning
5 flakes garlic (chopped finely)
salt and pepper to taste

Melt butter over low heat. Remove from heat and add milk and cheese. Return to heat and bring to a boil, stirring continuously until sauce thickens. Add chopped garlic, salt and pepper. Mix well.

CHILI SAUCE

1 cup chili powder
1 1/2 cups vinegar
3 tsp. ginger and garlic paste

2 tsp. oil
2 tbs. sugar
salt to taste

Put all the ingredients in a blender and blend well.

HOT AND SWEET SAUCE

1/4 cup tomato puree
1 tbs. grated onion
1/2 tsp. garlic paste
1/2 tsp. green chili paste
1/4 tsp. black pepper
1/2 tsp. chili powder

3/4 tbs. sugar
1/2 tbs. cornflour mixed with
 2 tbs. water
1 tbs. oil
1/3 cup water
salt to taste

Heat oil. Add the ginger, garlic, and green chili paste. Stir and add the onions. Fry on a low flame for about two minutes. Add the tomato puree, water, black pepper, chili powder, sugar, and salt. Bring to a boil and stir. Cook covered on a low flame for two minutes. Add the cornflour mixed with water and stir continuously till the sauce thickens. Serve with soups main dishes and snacks.

Breakfast Dishes

IDLI

4 cups raw rice (long grain)
1 cup urad dal (skinless,
  split black gram)

1 cup beaten rice (poha)
salt to taste

Soak the raw rice and urad dal separately for three hours. Grind urad dal to a fine paste. Grind the washed rice and the soaked beaten rice also to a fine paste. Mix both with salt to taste, adding the required amount of water to form a thick pouring consistency. Pour into greased idli steamer. Steam cook till soft and spongy for about 15-20 minutes. Serve with chutney and sambar.

MANGALORE IDLI

2 1/2 cups boiled rice (Uncle Ben's)
1/4 cup urad dal
  (skinless, split black grain)

1/2 cup raw rice (long grain)
1/2 tsp. yeast
1 tsp. sugar

Wash and soak the boiled rice, raw rice and urad dal together for 6 hours. Grind to a fine paste. Add salt, 1/2 tsp. yeast (soaked in 1 tsp. sugar and 1/4 cup warm water for 5 minutes) and remaining sugar. Add enough water to make pouring consistency. Leave to ferment for 4-5 hours or overnight. Pour into greased idli steamer and steam cook till soft and spongy for 15-20 minutes. Serve with chicken curry.

RAVA IDLI

2 cups semolina or rava
3 cups sour yogurt
2 tsp. bengal gram
1 tsp. urad dal
1 tsp. mustard seeds
1 cup grated coconut
1 large onion (chopped finely)

5 green chilies
1 tsp. ginger (chopped finely)
1/2 cup coriander leaves,
  chopped
1/2 tsp. baking soda
1/4 cup oil
salt to taste

Roast semolina in 1 tbs. oil. Heat the remaining oil, add mustard seeds, chopped green chilles, onions, urad dal, and channa dal, and fry till brown. Cool and add to semolina. Next, add grated coconut, coriander, ginger, baking soda, yogurt, and salt to taste. Beat well to form a thick batter. Pour into greased idli steamer and steam till soft and spongy for 15-20 minutes. Serve with vegetable korma.

MYSORE IDLI

150 gms. vermicelli

250 gms. semolina

10-15 cashewnuts

8-10 green Chilies

1 cup fresh grated coconut

1/2 cup coriander leaves chopped

1 tsp. urad dal

1 tsp. channa dal

1 tsp. mustard seeds

1/2 tsp. asafoetida

1 sprig curry leaves

1 liter yogurt

2 tbs. sugar

1/2 cup oil

1 tbs. baking soda

salt to taste

Roast semolina and vermicelli in 2 tbs. oil, separately till light brown and let it cool. Heat the remaining oil, add mustard seeds, green Chilies, urad dal, channa dal, and fry till brown. Add asafoetida and remove from heat. Add the roasted semolina and vermicelli, baking soda, grated coconut, coriander leaves, and cashewnuts. Add the beaten yogurt, sugar and salt and leave aside for half-hour. Mix and pour into greased idli steamer for 15-20 minutes until done. Serve with chutney and vegetable korma.

COCONUT CREAM IDLI

4 cups rice
  1/2 cup boiled rice
  (half cooked and cooled)
2 tbs. urad dal

1 tsb. yeast (soaked in 2 tsp.
  warm water and milk
  extracted from 1 whole
  coconut and 1 tsp. sugar
4 tsp. sugar
salt to taste

Wash and soak the rice and urad dal for three hours. Grind this along with the half cooked boiled rice and coconut milk till fine. Add the soaked yeast, salt, and remaining sugar. Stir and keep aside to ferment for 4-5 hours. Pour into greased idli steamer and steam for five to 10 minutes until done. Serve with coconut chutney.

ADAI

1 cup rice
1/2 cup urad dal
1/2 cup channa dal
1" piece ginger
10 sprigs of coriander leaves

1/2 cup moong dal
1/2 cup tuvar dal
6-8 green Chilies
2 onions

Soak together the rice and all the dals for 4-5 hours. Grind along with Chilies and ginger coarsely. Add the finely chopped onions and coriander and keep aside for 1 hour. Add salt to taste. Smear oil on pan and proceed to prepare just as you would cook dosas. Cook till crisp and serve hot with chutney.

GUNDU PONGAL

2 cups urad dal
4 cups semolina
4-5 green Chilies
1 piece ginger
 (chopped finely)

3 onions (chopped finely)
1/2 cup coriander leaves,
 chopped
1/2 cup oil
salt to taste

Soak urad dal for 2 hours. Grind to a fine paste. Add semolina and remaining ingredients, except oil. Mix well and enough water to form idli consistency. Smear the gundu pongal griddle with oil. Pour a spoonful of batter into each depression. Cover and cook on slow fire. (If you do not have a gundu pongal griddle, use an ordinary cast iron griddle pouring spoonfuls of batter 3" apart. Remove lid, turn the pongal and cook this side till brown and remove. Serve hot with chutney.

NEER DOSA
(A MANGALOREAN SPECIALITY)

2 cups rice
2 tbs. grated coconut

2 tbs. oil
salt to taste

Wash and soak the rice for two hours. Add coconut and grind to a very fine paste. Dilute the paste with water to form a thin consistency, thin enough to coat a spoon. Smear oil on the pan. Pour a spoonful and turn the pan till it spreads evenly. Cook it only on one side. Remove and let cool and then fold it twice into a triangular shape. Serve with chutney or chicken curry.

BREAD DOSA

2 cups rice
1/3 cup urad dal

2 slices bread
1 tsp. fenugreek seeds

Wash and soak rice, urad dal, and fenugreek seeds for 3-4 hours. Next, add the soaked bread and grind to a fine paste. Add enough water to make paste into dosa consistency and leave aside to ferment over night. Add salt to taste and make thick dosas. Cook on both sides till done. Serve hot with chutney.

MASALA DOSA

2 cups rice	1 cup channa dal
1 cup urad dal	1 tsp. fenugreek seeds

Wash and soak rice, dals, and fenugreek seeds for 3-4 hours. Grind to a fine paste and leave aside to ferment for 4-5 hours. Add salt to taste and make dosas. Serve hot with chutney and potato bhaji.

RAVA DOSA

2 cups rice flour	1 medium onion
1 cup rava	(chopped finely)
2 tbs. all purpose flour	1/4 cup coriander leaves
6-8 green Chilies	(chopped finely)
1 tsp. cumin	1 cup oil for frying
	salt to taste

Mix all ingredients to form a pouring consistency. Add salt to taste. Smear oil on the pan. Pour a spoonful of batter on the pan and tilt the pan to spread the batter. Serve hot with chutney.

RAGI DOSA

2 cups ragi flour
1/2 cup wheat flour
1/2 cup urad dal
1 tsp. fenugreek

1 cup butter milk
1/2 cup oil
salt to taste

Soak methi and urad dal for 3-4 hour. Grind to a fine paste. Mix in both the flours and butter milk. Add salt to taste. Set aside to ferment for 3 hours. Mix the batter well to form a pouring consistency. Smear oil onto a pan. Pour the batter and cook on both sides till crisp. Serve with coconut chutney.

SOORNALI

2 cups rice
1 cup beaten rice (poha)
2 cups butter milk
1 cup sugarcane juice or jaggery

1/2 cup fresh grated coconut
2 tsp. turmeric powder
salt to taste

Wash and soak rice along with poha and butter milk for 4-5 hours. Grind this to a fine paste. Add the grated coconut, sugarcane juice or jaggery, and salt and mix well. Set aside to ferment for 4-5 hours or overnight. Make dosas. Cover and cook only on one side. Serve hot with chutney and vegetable curry.

APPAM

2 cups rice
1 tbs. urad dal
1/2 cup coconut grated
1/2 cup beaten rice (poha)
1/2 tsp. yeast (dissolved in 1/4
  cup warm water and 1 tsp. sugar)

2 tbs. sugar
1/2 cup oil
salt to taste

Soak the rice and urad dal for 3-4 hours. Add grated coconut and beaten rice and grind finely to a thin paste. Add dissolved yeast, sugar, and salt to taste and leave to ferment for 4-5 hours or overnight. Smear oil on an appam pan or kadai. Pour a cupful and cook till done.

JHATPAT DOSA

2 cups rice	1 onion
1/2 cup freshly grated coconut	4 dry red chilies
1 tbs. coriander seeds	jaggery
1/2 tbs. cumin	salt to taste

Soak rice for 1 hour. Grind to a fine paste along with the rest of the ingredients. Smear oil and pour batter to make dosas. Serve with chutney.

MOONG DOSA

1 cup whole green gram or moon dal	1/2" piece ginger
1 tbs. rice	1 tsp. salt
2 dry red chilies	1/2 cup oil

Wash and soak the dal and rice for 10 hours or overnight. Drain and grind along with the other ingredients (except oil) adding 1 cup water. Heat pan on a medium fire and grease lightly. Pour one big spoonful of batter and spread lightly. Add 1 tsp. oil Cook till done. Serve hot with ginger pickle or chutney.

BENNE DOSA

2 cups rice
1/2 cup urad dal
1/4 cup channa dal
1/4 cup whole wheat

1 tbs. fenugreek seeds
oil for frying
salt to taste

Wash and soak rice, urad dal, channa dal, wheat, and fenugreek seeds for 4-5 hours. Grind together to form a fine paste. Add salt to form a semi thick batter. Cover and keep aside for 8 hours. Grease the pan and make dosas. When slightly brown add a spoonful of potato bhaji and a blob of butter to the center of the dosa. Immediately fold and cook till crisp. Serve with chutney.

PEAS PARATHAS

For the Stuffing
2 cups boiled green peas
5 green chilies
  (chopped finely)
1 tsp. cumin seeds
1 tbs. clarified butter (ghee)
clairfied butter for frying
salt to taste

For the dough
3 cups wheat flour
2 tbs. clairfied butter (ghee)
1/2 tsp. salt

Add clarified butter (ghee), enough water and salt to the flour and knead to form a soft dough. Mash the boiled green peas. Heat clarified butter (ghee) and fry cumin seeds and add green chilies. Fry for 1 min and add the mashed peas and salt to taste. Take a small portion of the dough and flatten it a little and add a tbs. of stuffing in the center. Cover and roll to form parathas. Cook on a hot pan with a little clarified butter (ghee) until brown patches appear. Serve hot with curry, pickles, and yogurt.

ALU BATURA

200 gms. flour
500 gms. potatoes boiled
  and mashed
1 tsp. chili powder

water
oil for frying
salt to taste

Sieve the flour. Add salt, chili powder, and potatoes and mix well, adding enough water to form a pliable dough. Set aside for 1/2 hour. Divide into balls, and roll them into big puris. Fry in hot oil till they puff up. Serve hot with channa masala.

Rice
Dishes

COCONUT RICE

2 cups rice
2 cups coconut milk
2 onions, sliced
1 tbs. cashewnuts
2 tbs. clarified butter (ghee)

1 tbs. mustard seeds
2 tsp. cloves and cinnamon
1/2 tsp. turmeric
curry leaves
salt to taste

Wash and soak rice for 1/2 hour. Extract two cups of coconut milk from fresh coconut. Heat clarified butter (ghee) and fry sliced onions till golden brown and remove on paper. Add the spices to the remaining clarified butter (ghee) and add drained rice and fry a little. Add turmeric powder, coconut milk, and salt to taste. Cover and cook till rice is done. Remove excess moisture by keeping in the oven for a few minutes. Garnish with fried onions and cashewnuts.

PLAIN PULAO

1 kg. rice (4 1/2 cups)
3 tbs. ginger and garlic paste
2 pieces of clove
2 pieces cinnamon
4-5 green chilis
2 pods cardamom

1/2 cup coriander leaves
2 onions, sliced
2 chilies
1/2 cup mint leaves
8 cups very hot water
salt to taste

Wash and soak rice for 1/2 hour. Heat clarified butter (ghee). Add the spices and fry till brown. Add the sliced onions and fry again. Add the ginger and garlic paste. Add the drained rice and fry a little. Then add the slit chilies, finely chopped coriander, and mint leaves. Add enough water, salt to taste, and cook till done. Serve with any curry.

CHINESE FRIED RICE

1/2 cup oil or butter
3 cups rice
1 kg. or 4 1/2 cups carrots
  (chopped finely)
1/2 kg. or 2 1/4 cups fresh
  peas (shelled)
2 tsp. white pepper powder
1 tbs. chili sauce
1 tsp. soy sauce or vinegar

5 cups boiling water
1/4 tsp. ajinomoto (optional)
1/2 kg. or 2 1/4 cups
  beans (cut finely)
1/2 kg cabbage
  (shredded finely)
4-5 spring onions, chopped
1" piece ginger grated
salt to taste

Cook the rice with salt till done. Spread in a plate and leave to cool. Heat oil or butter. Add ginger, onions, and all the vegetables one by one. Fry till half done and crisp. Add salt, ajinomoto, chili sauce, and soy sauce. Then add rice and stir well. Serve hot with chopped chili in vinegar and soy sauce.

CHICKEN BIRYANI (GREEN)

1 large chicken
Masala
45 green Chilies
4 big onions, chopped
1 whole bulb garlic
2" piece ginger
2 tbs. coriander seeds
1 tbs. poppy seeds
3-4 sprigs mint leaves
2 cups coriander leaves
2 cardamoms
20 cloves
4 pieces cinnamon
1 tsp. saffron
1 tsp. butter
juice of 1 lemon
salt to taste

Rice
1 kg basmati rice
1/4 kg clarified butter (ghee)
8 onions (sliced finely)
20 almonds
2 pieces of cinnamon
2 cardamoms
10 cups hot water
salt to taste

31

Clean and cut the chicken into large pieces. Grind all the masala ingredients to a paste without water. Add ground masala, and salt to the chicken. Cook till done. Add lime juice and remove from fire. Wash and drain rice. Heat clarified butter (ghee). Fry half of the onion and set aside. Fry almonds and set aside. Add the garam masala, fry a little and add the remaining sliced onions. Fry till half brown. Add drained rice and fry till crisp. Add ten cups of hot water, salt to taste, and cook on slow fire till done. In a flat vessel add clarified butter (ghee). Spread a layer of chicken mixture, then a layer of cooked rice. Then layer with fried onions and a few almonds. Repeat till everything is layered alternately. Garnish with fried onions or almonds. Cover with lid sealing edges with aluminum foil so that steam does not escape and cook for 10 minutes. Serve with onions and tomato salad.

VANGI MASALA BHAT

3 cups rice
1/4 kg. or 5 small eggplants
50 gms. cashewnuts
2 tbs. yogurt
1/2 cup fresh grated coconut
1/4 cup oil
1 tsp. mustard seeds
1/4 tsp. asafoetida powder

1/2 tsp turmeric powder
1 sprig curry leaves
2 green chilies
1 tbs. masala (coriander
  seeds, cumin, cinnamon,
  cloves, black cumin,)
  ground to powder

Wash and soak rice for 1 hour. Slit the eggplant into fourths. Heat the oil and season with mustard seeds, asafoetida, and turmeric. Add curry leaves, chilies, and eggplant. Add rice and fry for sometime. Add 6 cups boiled water, salt, chili powder, dry masala, cashewnuts, and yogurt. Cook on a slow fire. Serve hot with grated coconut and coriander leaves.

BISE BELE BHATH

1 tbs. clarified butter (ghee)
1 cup tuvar dal
2 cups basmati rice
1 cup beans, cut into 2"pieces
6 dry red chilies
1 tsp. pepper
1/2 tsp. cumin seeds
1/4 tsp. fenugreek seeds
4 tbs. urad dal
2 tbs. channa dal
4 cloves
4 long cinnamon
1/2 cup dry coconut flakes
1 lemon sized tamarind
1/4 tsp. turmeric powder

Seasoning
4 tbs. oil
4 red chilies
1 tsp. mustard seeds
1 tsp. bengal gram dal
1 tsp. urad dal
1/2 cup cashewnuts pieces
2 sprig curry leaves

In 5 cups of water, boil the tuvar dal with clarified butter (ghee) and turmeric powder. When the dal is just cooked, add washed rice, 3 cups of water, tamarind pulp, beans, and continue to cook. Roast the red chilies and the rest of the masala ingredients in a tsp. of oil. Grind this to a fine powder with dry coconut flakes. When rice is half cooked, add the masala powder and mix well. Cook till done. Heat 4 tbs. of oil. Add red chilies, bengal gram dal, urad dal, cashewnut pieces, mustard, and curry leaves. Pour the seasoning into the cooked rice and mix well. Finally add 1 tbs. of clarified butter (ghee) for flavor and serve.

MEXICAN VEGETABLE RICE

3 tbs. oil or refined oil
1 large onion chopped
4 cloves garlic, sliced
1 1/2 cups rice boiled and
 drained
250 gms. or 2 cups vegetables
 (peas, carrots, beans)

1/2 tsp. chili powder
3 chicken or vegetable
 soup cubes
1 cup chopped tomatoes
1 cup boiling water
salt to taste

In a wide frying pan, heat oil on medium heat. Add garlic and onions and fry till brown. Stir in chili powder, salt, and soup cubes dissolved in boiling water. Add vegetables and simmer till liquid is partially absorbed. Add rice and chopped tomatoes. Toss and retain on heat for 3 minutes till water is absorbed and dry. Serve hot with sauce and raitha.

PRAWN BIRYANI

2 cups shelled prawn
2 cups rice (half cooked)
3 tbs. melted butter
1/4 tsp. saffron powder
1/2 tsp. yellow coloring
2 medium onions
 (chopped finely)
1 cup oil
1 medium can, tomatoes or
 3 fresh tomatoes
10 small boiled and peeled potatoes

Masala Powder
3/4 tsp. cumin seeds
1/4 tsp. turmeric
1 tsp. ginger and garlic paste
1 tsp. chili paste
1 tsp. garam masala
coriander leaves, chopped
salt to taste

Heat the oil and fry the potatoes till golden brown. In same oil, fry onions till they reach a golden brown. Remove surplus oil, saving a little. Add the prawns, salt, and masala and fry for about 2-3 minutes. Add tomatoes and simmer till prawns are cooked. Next, add the potatoes and the saffron. Remove from heat. Spread rice in a layer on top of the prawn masala. Spread the food coloring and butter all over the rice. Place pan in a moderately hot oven for 15 minutes. Reduce heat slightly and continue to cook for 15 minutes. Serve hot with yogurt salad.

HYDERABADI BIRYANI

1-1 1/2 kg. (3 lbs.) mutton or
  lamb cleaned and cubed
4 cups basmati rice
2 cups clarified butter (ghee)
  or refined oil
2 1/2 tbs. ginger and garlic paste
4-5 medium onions (sliced finely)
1 tsp. garam masala, ground
juice of two small lemons
1 tsp. red chili powder

1/2 tsp. turmeric powder
1 tbs. chopped coriander
  leaves
1 tbs. chopped mint leaves
1 tbs. each of pepper corns,
  cloves, green cardamoms,
  and cinnamon sticks
1 tsp. saffron strands
salt to taste

Heat 2/3 of the clarified butter (ghee) and fry the sliced onions till golden brown. Set aside. In the same oil, add the meat, yogurt, red chili powder, turmeric, garam masala, and cardamoms. Add salt and the coarsely ground fried onions. Once the meat is cooked, add the lemon juice. Wash the rice and half cook it in salted water along with chopped mint, coriander, green chilies, and whole garam masala. Drain and set aside. Layer the rice and meat alternatively in a deep vessel finishing with the rice. Sprinkle the saffron strands and pour the remaining ghee or oil. Cover tightly and steam the biryani till done on a slow flame.

NAVARATHNA PULAO

2 1/2 cups basmati rice
250 grams (10 oz.) paneer, cubed
1 tsp. turmeric
1 cup hot water
1/4 cup almonds, blanched
  and sliced
2 onions (sliced thinly)
1 tsp. garlic (chopped finely)
2 tsp. ginger, sliced
4 cardamom
2" cinnamon
5 cloves

10 pepper corns
1 cup cauliflower cut into
  flowerets
1/2 cup shelled peas
4 cups water
2 tbsp. pistachio blanched
1/4 cup sultanas or
  white raisens
clarified butter (ghee)
oil for frying
salt to taste

Deep fry paneer cubes until golden and soak in hot water mixed with turmeric for 5 minutes. Remove and drain. Next, fry almonds in oil until golden and drain. Heat clarified butter (ghee) and fry cinnamon, cloves, cardamom, and pepper corns. Add onions and fry till golden brown. Next, add the ginger and garlic and fry for a few more minutes. Add cauliflower and peas and fry for 2 minutes. Add the rice and fry for 3 more minutes. Add water and cook covered till done for about 25 minutes. Remove from heat, add the paneer, almonds, pistachio, and sultanas. Mix well and serve with curry.

Vegetarian Curries

VEGETABLE KOOTU

1/2 cup channa dal
3/4 cup grated coconut
1/2 tsp. rice
1/2 tsp. cumin seeds
3-4 green chilies
1 tsp. salt
1/4 tsp. turmeric
250 gms. (1 1/4 cups)
  mixed vegetables

Seasoning
1/2 tsp. mustard seeds
2-3 tbs. oil
1-2 red chilies
curry leaves

Cook channa dal till it becomes soft. Any of the following vegetables (snake gourd, eggplant, white pumpkin, and a variety of beans, green banana, cabbage, or yam) can be used (single or in combination). Cut all the vegetables into small pieces and boil in just enough water with salt and turmeric. Grind coconut, cumin, chilies, and rice in a little water and add to the vegetables. Add boiled dal, and boil for 4-5 minutes. Sauté the seasonings in oil and add to the vegetable dal and mix. Serve hot with chappatis or rice.

NAVARATHNA CURRY

1 cup carrots
1 cup potatoes
1 cup beans
1 cup cauliflower
1 cup peas
1 cup beetroot
1/2 cup raisins
1/2 cup cashewnuts
1 1/2 cup coconut milk
1 cup apple, diced

Masala
2 green chilies, slit
2 tbs. oil
1/2 cup coriander leaves
  chopped
2 onions (chopped finely)
1 tsp. garam masala powder
1 tsp. coriander and cumin
  powder
1 tsp. pepper powder
salt to taste

Boil all the chopped vegetables. Heat oil. Add the finely chopped onions and fry till they become soft. Add garam masala, chili powder, coriander and cumin powder, and pepper powder. Fry a little and then add the boiled vegetables. Add coconut milk and salt and cook for 5 minutes. Remove from heat, and mix in chopped apples, raisins, fried cashewnuts. Garnish with chopped coriander and serve.

SPROUTED MOONG CURRY

1 kg sprouted moong beans
1 small onion

Masala
1/2 cup grated coconut
4-5 red chilies
1 tsp. coriander seeds roasted
1/2 tsp. cumin seeds
lemon sized tamarind or tomato

Seasoning
2 tbs. oil
1 tsp. mustard seeds
1 onion, chopped
1 sprig curry leaves
1/2 cup chopped coriander 1
salt to taste

Wash and sprout moong. Cook with onion and water till soft. Grind all the masala ingredients to a fine paste and add to the cooked gram. Boil for 5-10 min. Season with mustard seeds, onions, and curry leaves. Garnish with chopped coriander leaves.

POTATO CURRY

2 medium potatoes, cubed
clarified butter (ghee) for frying
1/2 tsp. cumin seeds
1 large onion, chopped
2 green chilies, slit
1/4 tsp. turmeric powder

1/2 tsp. red chili powder
2 ripe tomatoes
 (chopped finely)
1 tsp. chopped cashewnuts
1 cup cream (malai)
salt to taste

Marinate the potato pieces in salt and keep aside for sometime. Deep fry in ghee and remove. Melt 2 tbs. clarified butter (ghee) in a pan. Add cumin seed and chopped onions and fry till brown. Add green chilies, turmeric powder, red chili powder, and salt to taste. Add chopped tomatoes and fry for sometime till it leaves the sides of the pot. Add the water and stir chopped coriander and fried cashewnuts. Then add the fried potatoes and garnish with cream (malai). Serve hot with chappatis or rice.

RAW BANANA CURRY

3 raw bananas (skinned and
  cut into pieces, and soaked
  in water)
1/2 lime sized tamarind

Masala
 1/2 coconut grated
6-8 roasted red chilies
1 tsp. coriander seeds roasted
1/4 tsp. cumin seeds
2 flakes garlic

Seasoning
2 tbs. oil
1 tsp. mustard seeds
1 sprig curry leaves
7-8 flakes garlic, crushed
1 red chili
salt to taste

Soak the tamarind in water. Cook the banana pieces in salt, tamarind juice and 2 cups of water. Grind all the masala ingredients to a paste and add to the cooked banana. Boil for 10-15 minutes. Heat the oil. Season with mustard seeds, crushed garlic, red chilies, and curry leaves. Serve hot with rice and chappatis.

BAKED CHANNA (CHICK PEAS)

1/2 kg. (2 1/2 cups) kabuli
  channa (boiled and mashed)
1 tsp. chili powder
3 tbs. butter
2 tbs. oil
1 onion cut into rings
1 tsp. cumin powder
juce of 1 lime
10-12 pieces potatoes,
  chopped and fried
salt to taste

Chutney:
1 bunch coriander leaves
7-8 green chilies
7-8 cloves of garlic
1 tbs. coriander powder
a few mint leaves
1 onion
1/2 cup tamarind juice

Blend all the ingredients in a blender. Mash the channa (chick peas) while hot. Add salt, chili powder, and lime juce to it. Grease a baking dish with oil. Add a layer of mashed channa. Spread 2 tsp. of chutney over it and place the fried potatoes and onion rings on top. Repeat with another layer of mashed channa and dot it with butter. Bake for 20 minutes and serve.

VEGETABLE AU GRATIN

1/4 kg potatoes, chopped
  and boiled
100 gms. or 1/2 cup
  beans, chopped
100 gms. or 1/2 cup
  carrots, chopped
150 gms. or 3/4 cup
  peas, boiled
3 cups white sauce*

1 tbs. chili sauce
1 cup grated cheese
2 tbs. worchester sauce
1 tbs. tomato ketchup
1 cup boiled macaroni
1 cup fresh cream
1/2 cup bread crumbs
2 tbs. butter
salt to taste

*See SAUSES & CHUTNEYS

Add salt, tomato ketchup, 1/2 cup grated cheese, chili sauce, and Worcester sauce and mix well. Add in the boiled vegetables, boiled macaroni, fresh cream, and white sauce. Fold into a greased baking dish. Cover with remaining grated cheese, and bread crumbs. Dot it with butter and bake till top is golden brown. Serve hot.

SHAHI PALAK KOFTA

Gravy
50 gms. or 1/2 cup cashewnuts
10 gms. or 1 tsp. poppy seed
1/2 tsp. chili powder
1/2 tsp. salt
1/2 tsp. turmeric
1 tsp. garam masala
2 tbs. oil
1/2 cup fresh cream

480 gms. or 1 lb. spinach
225 gms. mashed potatoes
10 gms. gram flour (besan)

Kofta filling
20 gms. paneer
20 gms. coconut
10 gms. cornflour
5 gms. cashewnuts and raisins
   chopped coursely

Oil for deep frying koftas

Wash the spinach. Chop it finely. Combine gram flour, mashed potatoes, and spinach. Take small portions and form balls. Combine paneer, coconut, cashews, and raisins. Place a little of this mixture into the mashed pototo balls. Heat oil and fry the balls till brown and drain. Grind together cashewnuts, poppy seed, chili powder, turmeric, and garam masala. Heat oil and cook the gravy mixture on slow fire for ten minutes. Add salt. Just before serving, place the koftas in a dish. Pour gravy over the koftas. Garnish with cream and chopped coriander leaves.

GREEN CHILI CURRY

1/4 kg. green chilies
(the long variety)
1/2 cup oil
1/2 tsp. cumin seeds
1 tbs. coriander seeds
3 tbs. dessicated coconut
1/2 tsp. poppy seeds
1/2 tsp. turmeric powder
1/4 tsp. chili powder

1 tsp. ginger and garlic paste
lemon sized ball of tamarind

Seasoning
2 medium onion, sliced
1/2 tsp. cumin seeds
1/2 tsp. mustard seeds
a few curry leaves

Wash the chilies and slit them lengthwise with a sharp knife. Do not remove stems. Fry the chilies in hot oil for 5 minutes and keep aside. Roast cumin, coriander, coconut, poppy seeds, and onion separately and grind to a fine paste. In the same oil add sliced onions, cumin seeds, and curry leaves. Add ground paste, turmeric ginger, ginger paste, and chili powder and fry till oil floats. Add fried chilies, tamarind juice and required amount of water and cook for a few minutes.

BAGHARA BAINGAN

450 gms. or 1 lb. small eggplant
1 cup oil
1 tsp. red chili powder
1/2 tsp. turmeric
3 tsp. coriander powder
11/2 tsp. poppy seeds
11/2 tsp. sesame seeds
2 tbs. peanuts

1 tbs. coconut powder
50 gms. or 2 oz. tamarind
1 medium onion
1 tsp. cumin seeds
1/2 cup of water
few curry leaves
1 cup coriander leaves
salt to taste

Quarter the eggplants lengthwise leaving the stems intact. Roast poppy seeds, sesame seeds, peanuts, and 1/2 tsp. cumin seeds, and grind with the onions. Heat oil and put the other 1/2 tsp. of cumin seeds in until they crackle. Add the eggplant and fry evenly for two minutes. Remove the eggplant. In the remaining oil, fry the rest of the spices and ground masala except tamarind. Fry well for 10-15 minutes. Add the eggplant back to this gravy. Add water, curry leaves, and tamarind extract. Simmer gently till the eggplant is cooked. Serve hot, garnished with coriander leaves.

Non Vegetarian Dishes

GINGER CHICKEN

1 kg. or 2 1/4 lbs Chicken
  (approx. 8 pieces)
1/2 kg. onion
1 bunch coriander leaves
1 bunch mint
50 grams or 2 oz. green chilies
200 grams or 8 oz. ginger
50 grams or 2 oz. garlic
1/2 cup milk

1 cup oil
4-5 drops red food coloring
  (optional)
A pinch of ajinomoto
  (optional)
1 tbs. soy sauce
2 tsp. red chili powder
pinch of sugar
salt to taste

Clean the chicken and cut into pieces. Grind the onions, garlic, ginger and green chilies into a smooth paste. Heat oil. Add the paste and fry till it turns golden brown. Add chicken pieces and continue to fry for 10 more minutes. Add food coloring, red chili powder, soy sauce, ajinomoto, sugar and milk. Add salt to taste. Cook chicken until tender. Garnish with coriander and mint leaves.

CHILI CHICKEN

1 kg. or 2 1/4 lbs. chicken
150 grams or 6 oz. corn flour
2-3 eggs
50 grams or 2 oz. green chilies
50 grams or 2 oz. ginger
  and garlic paste
1 tsp. ajinomoto (optional)
1 tsp. pepper
1 1/2 tsp. soy sauce

3 cups chicken stock
(add pepper, salt, 1 tbs.
  vinegar, 2 tbs. chopped
  onions and 2 bay leaves to
  chicken stock and boil)
chopped coriander leaves
oil for deep frying
salt to taste

Clean and cut chicken into small pieces. Make a mixture of beaten eggs, 100 grams corn flour, 1/2 tsp. ajinomoto, 1/2 tsp. pepper and salt. Marinate the chicken in this mixture for about an hour. Deep fry the chicken and drain. In a pan, heat 2 tbs. oil.

Add finely chopped green chilies and fry. Next add ginger and garlic paste and chopped coriander leaves. Add the chicken stock and the fried chicken pieces to the pan. Dissolve the remaining corn flour in water and add to the chicken. Finally, add remaining ajinomoto, pepper powder and soy sauce and simmer till done.

BADAM CHICKEN

1 kg. or 2 1/4 lbs.chicken,
  cleaned and cut into large pieces
1 inch piece ginger
5 cloves of garlic
10 green chilies
1 tsp. cumin seeds

1 bunch of coriander leaves
15 almonds
milk extracted from 1
  whole coconut
2 tbs. oil or clarified butter

Boil the chicken with chopped ginger and salt to taste. Grind the garlic, cumin seeds, green chilies and coriander leaves to a fine paste. Grind the almonds separately to a fine paste. Heat oil and fry the green masala paste till brown. Add the chicken pieces along with the almond paste and fry for a minute. Add the coconut milk, cover and cook on a low fire till chicken is tender.

FRIED CHICKEN

1 kg. or 2 1/4 lbs. boneless chicken
  (cut into medium sized pieces)
3 tbs. vinegar
1 tsp. lemon juice
oil for deep frying

4 tbs. red chili powder
1/2 tsp. turmeric powder
red food coloring (optional)
2 tsp. ginger and garlic paste

Marinate the chicken in a mixture of all of the above ingredients, (except oil) for half an hour. Boil chicken till almost cooked. Strain. Deep fry in hot oil. Serve garnished with onion and lemon slices. *Chicken pieces can also be grilled rather than fried.

CHICKEN MADURA

1 kg. or 2 1/4 lbs. chicken
25 grams or 1 oz.
  poppy seeds (khus-khus)
2 tsp. cumin seeds
4 cloves of cardamom
50 grams or 2 oz. cashew nuts
1 cup curd (yogurt)
red food coloring (optional)
salt and pepper to taste
oil for frying

Grind all of the ingredients with salt and pepper to a fine paste. Marinate the chicken pieces for 2 hours. Heat oil and deep fry the chicken pieces. Serve with onion and lemon slices.

CHICKEN IN BREAD CRUMBS

6 chicken breast pieces
100 gms or 4 oz. cheese, grated
6 tbs oil
50 gms or 2 oz. butter
1 egg, beaten
salt and pepper to taste
1 cup bread crumbs

White sauce
300 ml or 1 1/4 cups milk
50 grams or 2 oz. butter
40 grams or 1 1/2 oz.
  all-purpose flour
a pinch of nutmeg powder
salt and pepper to taste

Make white sauce by melting the butter in a saucepan. Add flour and cook for 1 minute, stirring constantly. Remove from heat and gradually add milk. Mix well to a smooth consistency. Return to heat and simmer, stirring constantly until sauce thickens. Season with salt, pepper, and nutmeg powder. Set aside to cool. Beat the egg. Dip chicken pieces in white sauce and then in the beaten egg. Coat with breadcrumbs and shallow fry the chicken pieces. Grease a baking dish with 50 grams butter and arrange the fried chicken in a layer. Pour the remaining white sauce over it. Sprinkle grated cheese and bake in a 350°F oven until cheese melts.

CHICKEN TIKKA

1 kg. or 2 1/4 lbs.
 boneless chicken
1/2 cup yogurt
1 tbs. lemon juice
1 1/2 tbs. chili powder

2 tsp. ginger and garlic paste
4 green chilies
1 bunch coriander leaves
1 bunch mint leaves
salt to taste

Cut chicken into small pieces. Grind remaining ingredients. Marinate chicken in this mixture for 6-8 hours. Insert into skewers and grill, or cook in oven until done. Serve with chutney and lemon wedges.

CHICKEN PIE

1 cup cooked and shredded
 chicken
1 cup all-purpose flour
1/2 cup fine semolina
1/2 cup orange juice
2 tbs. raisins

1 egg white
2 tbs. grated cheese
2 tbs. butter
salt to taste

Marinate chicken in orange juice and raisins for a few minutes. Adding a pinch of salt, butter, and a little water, knead the all-purpose flour and semolina into a soft dough. Divide this into 2 portions and roll to form 2 large pancakes. Grease a pie plate and press one pancake into it. Spread the marinated chicken over dough. Sprinkle grated cheese and cover with other pancake pressing lightly all around. Brush with egg white and bake until golden brown. Cut into slices. Can be served hot or cold.

CANTONESE CHICKEN

1 kg. or 2 1/4 lbs. chicken,
  boneless
6 pods garlic (crushed)
15-20 chilies (chopped)
2 onions
4 tbs. refined oil

1 tsp. cornflour
2 tsp. soy sauce
1 tsp. vinegar
1/2 tsp. pepper powder
1/2 tsp. turmeric powder

Clean chicken and cut into small pieces. To this, add soy sauce, vinegar, turmeric, 2 pods crushed garlic, and salt to taste. Boil until pieces are cooked and tender. Drain pieces, dissolve 1 tsp. cornflour to stock and keep aside. Heat oil in a pan, fry chicken pieces and remove. Heat 4 tbs. refined oil. Add remaining crushed garlic, chilies, and onions and fry until brown. Pour chicken stock, ajinomoto (optional), pepper, and salt. Let simmer for 2 minutes. Serve with fried rice.

CHICKEN BUTTER FRY

1 kg. or 2 1/4 lbs. chicken pieces
2 onions chopped
1 cup breadcrumbs
1 egg
oil
2 tomatoes (chopped)

Masala
15 green chilies
1 tsp. peppercorn
2 inch piece ginger
2 pods garlic
1/2 tsp. turmeric powder
salt to taste

Grind masala ingredients. Cook chicken pieces in it. Add chopped onions and tomatoes and cook without adding water. Add breadcrumbs and mix well. Dip chicken pieces in beaten egg and fry until golden brown.

CHICKEN FRY

1 kg. or 2 1/4 lbs. chicken
10 red chilies
1 tsp. pepper
1 tsp. Khus Khus
3 inch piece cinnamon
6 cloves
3 cardamoms

1 tsp. jeera
1 tbs. coriander leaves
2 inch piece copra
(dessicated coconut)
2 tsp. salt
4 tsp. ghee

Fry all masala ingredients in 2 tsp. ghee. Grind into fine paste with salt. Cut chicken into big pieces and marinate in masala for 2 hours. Heat oil or ghee and fry pieces by constantly stirring until done. Do not add water.

CHICKEN MANCHURIAN

1 kg. or 2 1/4 lbs. chicken
200 grams or 8 oz. cornflour
3 eggs
8 green chilies chopped
3 pods garlic chopped
1/4 cup chicken stock

1 tsp. ajinomoto (optional)
1 tsp. pepper powder
1 1/2 tsp. soy sauce
3 bunches coriander chopped
oil to fry
salt to taste

Mix 150 grams cornflour, beaten egg, 1/2 tsp. ajinomoto, 1/2 tsp. pepper powder, and salt. Mix chicken pieces in this paste and deep fry pieces in oil. Heat oil in pan, add chopped garlic and fry. Add coriander and green chilies. Add a little chicken stock, and allow to cook. Add remaining cornflour mixed in water, ajinomoto, pepper powder, salt, and soy sauce. Fry until crisp.

TANDOORI CHICKEN

1 kg. or 2 1/4 lbs. chicken
2 cups curds (yogurt)
2 tbsp. Ginger
2 tbsp. Coriander powder
1 tsp. red Chili powder

1 tsp. turmeric powder
10 drops red color (optional)
1 tbsp. Cumin powder
1 tsp. butter
salt to taste

Make deep cuts over the breast and legs of the chicken. Mix all ingredients in curds except red coloring. Smear chicken with mixture and marinate for 10-12 hours. Bake in 450° F oven for 10 minutes. Remove from oven and smear with mixture of red Chili powder, cumin powder, red food coloring, and butter. Broil for 5 minutes or until surface of chicken turns golden brown.

MASALA CHILI CHICKEN

1 kg. or 2 1/4 lbs. chicken
15 red chilies
2 tbs. coriander powder
1/2 tsp. turmeric powder
2 tbs. lime juice

4 onions chopped
2 pods garlic chopped
4 tbs. oil
salt and pepper to taste

Grind coriander powder, red chilies, and turmeric powder into a paste. Marinate chicken pieces in this paste and add 2 tbs. lime juice and pepper powder. Boil until done. Heat oil or ghee. Add chopped onions and garlic and fry. Add chicken pieces, mix and serve hot.

CRISPY FRIED CHICKEN

1 kg. or 2 1/4 lbs. chicken
  (cleaned and cut into pieces)
1 tbs. ginger and garlic paste

Batter
1 tbs. all-purpose flour
2 tbs. cornflour
1 egg beaten
1/2 tsp. ajinomoto (optional)
1/2 tsp. soy sauce
1 tsp. Worcestershire sauce
1 tsp. vinegar
1/2 tsp. salt

Par boil chicken pieces in 2 cups water, 1/2 tsp. salt, and 1 tbs. tsp. ginger and garlic paste. Remove pieces, keep aside the stock. Beat all batter ingredients, if you find it thick, add 2 tbs. chicken stock. Heat oil, coat the chicken pieces with the batter and deep fry until golden brown. Drain on paper and serve.

*This batter can be used for prawns, cauliflower, or any other vegetable.

CHICKEN 65

1 kg. chicken or 2 1/4 lbs.
  cleaned and cut into large pieces)
Masala
20 red chilies
1 inch piece ginger
1 pod garlic
6 cloves
four 1 inch pieces cinnamon
1 tsp. turmeric

3 tbs. curds (yogurt)
1 egg
1 cup breadcrumbs
salt to taste
oil for frying

Grind all masala ingredients into fine paste. Beat curds and add ground masala, salt, and mix well. Marinate the chicken pieces for 1 hour. Cook chicken until half done. Beat the egg, dip the chicken in it. Roll chicken pieces in breadcrumbs. Deep fry in hot oil until golden brown.

CHICKEN LAJAWAB

1 kg. or 2 1/4 lbs. chicken
  (cleaned and cut into pieces)
2 cups milk
3 onions sliced very thin
3 tbs. almond paste
pinch of saffron soaked in a
  little warm milk
4 tbsp. butter
2 cups heavy cream
1/2 cup raisins
1/2 cup chicken stock
1 tbsp. ginger and garlic paste
4-6 green chilies
  (slit lengthwise)
4 cloves
4 small pieces cinnamon
2 whole brown cardamom
2 tbsp. chopped
  coriander leaves

Boil chicken pieces with enough water and salt until a quarter done. Reserve the stock and shred the chicken. Cook shredded chicken with milk until milk evaporates. Heat butter, add green chilies, cardamom, cinnamon, cloves, ginger garlic paste, and sliced onions. Fry until light brown. Add almond paste and fry until golden brown. Add raisins, salt, pepper to taste, and fry a little more. Arrange chicken in a greased baking dish in one layer. To the above cooked paste, add saffron, heavy cream, chicken stock, to form a thick sauce. Pour sauce over the chicken and bake in oven at 350°F until top of sauce turns light brown. Garnish with coriander leaves.

COUNTRY CAPTAIN

1 kg. or 2 1/4 lbs. chicken or
  mutton (boiled and cut
  into very small pieces)
2 onions chopped
1 tbsp. ginger garlic paste
2 eggs boiled
2 potatoes boiled and peeled
250 grams or 10 oz. cheese
1 tbs. sugar
salt to taste
2 tbsp. flour
30 grams or 1 1/2 oz. butter
1/2 cup bread crumbs
1 1/2 bunch coriander leaves
4 green chilies chopped
1 tsp. chili powder
1 tbs. vinegar
1 tbs. ghee

Heat ghee and add chopped onions and fry until brown. Add ginger garlic paste and fry a little. Add chicken pieces and fry a little. Add chopped green Chilies and a little water. Cook until chicken is done. Strain and reserve stock. Heat ghee in pan. Add 2 tbs. all-purpose flour and roast. Add chopped coriander and green Chilies and roast. Add Chili powder, shredded chicken, vinegar, and sugar. Cook until it thickens. Cut boiled potatoes and eggs into round shapes. Brown potatoes in a little oil. Grease a baking dish and layer chicken in bottom of dish. Cover with potato and egg slices. Sprinkle grated cheese and breadcrumbs. Dot with butter and bake in hot oven until top turns golden brown.

SHREDDED CHICKEN WITH CAPSICUM

1 1/2 cups shredded boneless chicken
1 small onion minced
2 tsp. ginger paste
2 capsicums seeded and sliced lengthwise
4 tsp. oil
pinch of sugar

Marinade
2 tbsp. Soy sauce
2-3 tbsp. oil
1/2 tsp. salt
1 tbsp. sherry
2 tsp. cornflour
1/4 tsp. ajinomoto (optional)
1 tsp. black pepper powder

Marinate the chicken in marinade mixture for 3 hours. Heat 2 tbs. oil in frying pan and add chicken. Stir fry for 2-3 minutes until dry, keep aside. Heat another 2 tbs. oil in pan. Add onions, ginger paste, and fry for a minute, add sliced capsicum and fry for another minute on high flame. Lower flame, add sugar and fried chicken, mix well. Serve hot. *Variation- Use sliced button mushrooms which have been sauteed in a little garlic butter instead of capsicum.

BAKED CHICKEN PIE

4cups shredded chicken
  (boiled with salt, pepper, and
  turmeric powder)
2 1/2 cups mayonnaise
1 cup finely chopped onions
1/2 cup finely chopped ginger,
  garlic and green chilies.
1/2 cup chopped mushrooms
1/2 cup finely chopped celery
1/2 cup cashew nuts chopped
1/2 cup coriander leaves
  chopped
1/2 of a lemon
1 cup crushed potato chips
1 cup grated cheese
3 tbs. ghee
oil for frying

In a bowl mix the shredded chicken, onions, ginger, garlic, green chilies, celery, and coriander leaves. Fry the mushrooms and cashew nuts in oil till brown. Add this to the rest of the ingredients. Mix in mayonnaise. Squeeze half a lemon over it. Add 3 tbs. ghee to the entire mixture and mix well. Take a flat dish or a pie pan and arrange this mixture in it. Flatten it with a knife so that the surface is smooth. Garnish with crushed potato chips and grated cheese. Bake it for about 20-25 minutes in a pre-heated oven at 220° F. Decorate with tomatoes. This dish can be served hot or cold with bread rolls.

CHICKEN ROLLS IN CREAMY SAUCE

1 kg. or 2 1/4 lbs.boneless chicken
250 grams yogurt (curds)
6-8 pepper corns
6 cloves garlic
4 cloves
1 black cardamom
4 green cardamoms
2 pieces of cinnamon
50 grams cashew nuts
salt to taste
1/2 cup cream
3-4 tbs. oil
green chilies to taste

Filling
1 onion
1 small piece ginger
2 green chilies
10-12 almonds
10-12 raisins
small bunch of coriander leaves

Wash the chicken pieces. Beat with the back of a knife to make them flat. Finely chop all of the ingredients for the filling. On each piece of the flattened chicken, put a little of the filling and roll up tightly. Tie with a white cotton string every 2" apart, taking care to keep the filling inside. Roll all the chicken pieces the same way. In a non-stick pan, add 3-4 tbs. of oil and fry the chicken rolls lightly. Cool. Remove string and cut into 1" pieces. Beat the yogurt and add to the chicken. To this, add chopped garlic, cloves, peeled black cardamom, green cardamom, cinnamom, pepper corns and salt to taste. Grind cashew nuts and green chilies to a fine paste. Add to the chicken and when tender, add cream. Sizzle once on high heat and serve hot with romali roti or naan.

KADAI CHICKEN

1 kg. or 2 1/4 lbs.chicken, thighs or breast cut into small pieces
1 tsp. salt
1 tsp. cumin seeds
1 1/2 tbs. chopped garlic
2-3 tbs. oil

4-5 medium tomatoes chopped
5-6 green chilies
1/2 -1 tsp. red chili powder
4 tbs. or 1 small bunch chopped coriander leaves

Heat oil and cumin seeds and chopped garlic. When it turns brown, add chicken pieces and salt. Cook over a high flame till all of the moisture evaporates. When dry, add tomatoes, green chilies, red chili powder and cook tomatoes till thick gravy is formed a oil separates. Finally add coriander leaves and serve hot with chappatis, paratha, or pulao rice. *You can also add 2 diced capsicum and 2 small bunches of methi leaves along with tomatoes and chilies. It gives a unique flavor.

MUGHLAI CHICKEN

1kg. 2 1/4 lbs. chicken
2 medium onions chopped finely
4 big tomatoes chopped finely
1/2 cup chopped coriander
  leaves
1 cup yogurt (curds)
3 green cardamoms
2 pieces of 1 inch cinnamon
3 cloves
4 tbs oil
salt to taste

Grind to paste
1 red onion
6 cloves garlic
1 tsp garam masala
1-1 1/2 tsp. red Chili powder
1/2 tsp. cumin powder
1/2 tsp. coriander seeds
15 cashew nuts

Clean chicken and cut into 12 pieces. Mix the ground paste with yogurt and marinate chicken with salt for 1/2 hour. Fry onions till light brown. Add the green cardamoms, cloves,and cinnamon sticks and fry for a minute. Add chopped tomatoes and the marinated chicken. Simmer on low flame until the chicken is cooked and a thick gravy forms. Serve hot garnished with coriander leaves.

CHICKEN ROAST

900 grams or 2 lbs. chicken
1 cup yogurt (curds)
1 tsp orange food colour
  (optional)
10 cloves of garlic
2 inches piece ginger
5 cloves

3 sticks cinnamon
1 tsp jeera
1 tsp coriander seeds
10 dry chilies
3 cardamoms
10 pepper corns
salt to taste

Grind all the ingredients into a fine paste. Marinate the chicken with the paste for 8 hours. Preheat oven and roast chicken at 400°F until it browns.

MANGALORE CHICKEN CURRY

1 kg or 4 1/4 lbs. chicken
  (cleaned and cut into
  medium pieces)
1 1/2 coconut grated
1/2 small coconut grated
20 red chilies, dry
2 tbs. coriander seeds
1 tsp. jeera (cumin)
1 tsp. methi (ferngreek) seeds
1 tbs. pepper corns
ghee for frying
1 onion chopped

1/2 tsp. turmeric powder
10 cloves garlic
1 onion chopped
1 tbs. butter
salt to taste
tamarind

Seasoning
2 tsp. ghee
1 onion chopped
1/2 tsp. garam masala
(cardamom, cloves, cinnamon)

Grate 1 1/2 coconuts and grind with hot water and extract
milk. Add 3 cups water to dilute coconut milk. Roast in s tbsp.
of ghee, dry red chilies, coriander, cumin, ferngreek seeds,
pepper corn and 1 chopped onion. To this add 1/2 grated
cocnut and roast until light brown. Grind to a paste. Boil chicken
with salt and butter and with ground masala, cook until chicken
is done. Add coconut milk, bring to boil. Simmer for 2 min.
Heat ghee in pan, add chopped onions. Fry until brown. Add
whole garam masala and pour over the curry. Serve with rice,
dosa, appa, or idli.

PATRA FISH

2 kg. any soft fleshed fish
  like pomfret or flounder
  (sliced and cleaned)
1 1/2-2 tsp. salt
Chutney
1 1/2 cup grated coconut
4 cups chopped coriander leaves
8-10 green chilies

1 1/2 tsp. cumin seeds
8-10 cloves garlic
2 1/2 tsp. sugar
2 1/2 -3 tsp. lemon juice

salt to taste
banana leaves or aluminum
foil cut into 5" squares

Clean fish and rub well with salt and keep aside. Grind to a paste all ingredients for chutney. Make as many pieces of foil or leaves as there are fish. Coat a slice of fish completely with prepared chutney. Coat one side of banana leaf with oil, and wrap fish in it securing with a toothpick. Repeat this with every piece of fish. Place wrapped fish pockets in a steamer and steam cook for 15-20 minutes or until fish is cooked.

FISH PIE

1/2 kg. or 1 1/4 lbs. sea fish*	1 medium onion diced
2 medium carrots	3/4 tsp. salt
15-20 french beans	3/4 tsp. pepper
5-6 florets cauliflower	1 1/2 inch ginger
1/2 cup peas	3-4 potatoes

Boil the fish with salt and keep aside. Boil potatoes and mash. Cut all vegetables into 1/4" bits and boil or steam them. Cut onions and ginger very finely. Fry onions in a little butter until soft. Add ginger, salt, and pepper. Add all vegetables and fish, mix and refrigerate for a while. Grease a baking tray, place fish mixture. Beat potatoes with a little milk and spread over the fish mixture. Sprinkle breadcrumbs and bake in a moderately hot oven until top browns. Serve hot.

FISH LOAF

250 grams or 10 oz. fish*	1/2 bunch coriander leaves
50 grams or 4 tbsp. butter	4 eggs
2 tbs. all-purpose flour	salt and pepper to taste
1/2 cup fresh cream	3/4 cup milk
1/2 tsp. garam masala	

*(eg., salmon, tuna, mackeral, pomfret)

Boil the fish, debone, and keep aside. Melt butter and roast flour a little. Add milk and boil until it thickens to make white sauce. Beat egg whites until stiff. Add yolks to it and beat well again. Add all remaining ingredients to it. Grease a bread loaf tin and pour mixture into it and bake in a moderately hot oven until done.

FISH MACKAREL PICKLE

8 mackarels (cleaned and
  cut into 4 pieces each)

Masala
40 red chilies
2 tbs. fenugreek seeds roasted
3 tbs. cumin seeds roasted

1 tbs. turmeric powder
salt to taste

1 bottle brown vinegar for
  grinding
4 tbs. mustard or refined oil
4 full garlic pods
  (cut into rounds)
1 1/2 pieces ginger
  (cut into rounds)
100 grams green chilies
  (cut into rounds)

Grind all masala ingredients in a little vinegar to fine paste. Mix mackarel pieces with turmeric powder and salt, keep aside for 15 min. Fry mackarel pieces in mustard oil until they become stiff and keep aside. In the same oil, fry garlic until brown and fry ginger and chilies too. Add ground masala with remaining vinegar to make thick paste. Fry thoroughly. Add fried mackarel pieces and let boil on slow fire until dry. Remove from fire, cool and store in glass jar.

PRAWN FRY WITH CHILI SAUCE

1 1/2 cups prawn
1 1/2 tbs. all-purpose flour
1 tsp. baking powder
1/2 tsp. ajinomoto (optional)
salt to taste

Chili sauce
1 cup chili powder
1 1/2 cup vinegar
3 tsp. ginger and garlic paste
salt to taste
2 tbs. sugar

Marinate prawns with all-purpose flour, baking powder, ajinomoto, and salt to taste for one hour. Deep fry in oil and remove. In a blender, add rest of ingredients to vinegar and blend well. Serve sauce with fried prawns.

MUTTON CHILI FRY

1/2 kg. or 1 1/4 lbs. mutton
20 grams or 3/4 oz. long
  thin green chilies
3 tbs. cornflour
20 grams or 2 tbs. onions
  (finely cut)
3 tbs. oil for cooking
1 cup yogurt
1 lemon

Masala
5 green chilies
5 pods garlic
1/4" piece fresh ginger
3 cloves
2 cardamoms
  (1 black and 1 green)

Marinate the mutton with the ground masala, 1 cup yogurt, and juice of 1 lemon for 1/2 or 1 hour. Cut the chilies into fine thin strips, remove seeds, soak them in water for 10 minutes to remove excess spice. Fry onions in 2 tbs. oil until golden brown. Add marinated mutton and fry until meat browns well. Add 1 1/2 glasses water to mutton and pressure cook for 15 min. until soft. Replace again on heat and add the slit chilies. Continue frying until all of the water has evaporated. Mix cornflour with 1 cup water and add to meat and cook till brown thickens. Garnish with fresh coriander and tomato wedges. Serve with naan, chopped spring onions, carrots, and cucumber.

MUTTON CHOPS

1 kg. or 2 1/4 lbs. mutton (lamb chops) beaten with mallet
1 1/2 tsp. ginger and garlic paste
1 tsp. garam masala
juice of 1 large lime
6-7 large onions cut into slices and sautéd
2-3 large potatoes cut into slices and fried

salt to taste
2 tbs. oil

Grind to a paste
6-8 green chilies
1 1/2 cups coriander leaves chopped
3/4 cup mint chopped

Marinate meat with salt, ginger garlic, ground paste, garam masala, and lemon juice. Pressure cook this meat for 10 min. on full pressure. Heat oil in shallow vessel. Pour contents of pressure cooker and simmer until liquid evaporates. Add potaotoes and sauteed onions and mix. Garnish with chopped coriander leaves and sliced boiled eggs (optional).

MEAT LOAF

500 grams or 1 1/4 lbs. kheema (ground lamb)
3 onions chopped finely
2 tbs. garlic powder
1 tbs. tomato sauce
4 slices bread (crumbled)

1 tsp. garam masala
1 tbs. Worcestershire sauce
salt and pepper to taste
2 eggs

Wash kheema and keep aside. Fry onions until brown. Add meat and sautee for some time. Add garlic powder and remaining ingredients. Mix well. Grease a loaf pan, pour mixture and press into the pan. Bake for 1/2 hour at 250° F until brown. Cool, and invert onto a plate. Garnish with onions, tomatoes, and lemon slices.

HARRICOT MUTTON

1/2 kg. or 1 1/4 lbs. mutton
2 medium onions chopped
2 tbs. Worcestershire sauce
1 1/2 tsp. ginger and garlic paste
1 tsp. pepper powder

1/2 tsp. ajinomoto (optional)
1 tin baked beans
100 grams potato chips
salt to taste
oil to fry

Fry onions until brown. Add ginger and garlic paste and mutton, fry until brown. Add Worcestershire sauce, salt, pepper and a little water and pressure cook until done. Add ajinomoto. Arrange meat in a flat dish. Top with a layer of baked beans. Garnish with crushed potato chips. Bake in a moderately hot oven for 20 minutes.

EGG MASALA

4 hard boiled eggs
1 large onion chopped fine
2 large tomatoes chopped
4 medium sized potatoes
  (boiled and peeled)
salt to taste
oil for frying
2 tbs. grated copra
  (dessicated coconut)
1 tsp. poppyseeds

masala
1/4 tsp. turmeric powder
6 red chilies
1 small onion
1/2 tsp. coriander powder
1/2 tsp. garam masala powder
1/4 tsp. brown sugar

Grind the masala ingredients to a smooth paste. Heat oil and fry onions until brown. Add masala and fry well. Add salt and water and cook for 2 min. Slit eggs lengthwise and cut potatoes into large cubes. Add this to the masala and simmer to form a thick sauce. Garnish with coriander and onion rings.

Snacks and Sweets

STUFFED DAHIVADA

100 grams 4 oz. urad dhal
  (skinless split black beans)
600 grams or 4 1/2 cups
  yogurt (beaten)
100 grams or 3/4 cup buttermilk
200 grams or 8 oz. potatoes
40 grams or 3 tbs. carrots cubed
40 grams or 3 tbs. peas

Masala for stuffing:
3-4 green chilies
small piece ginger
coriander leaves
25 grams or 2 tbs. dry fruit
salt to taste

Soak urad dhal for 4-5 hours. Grind to prepare a thick batter adding salt to taste. Pressure cook potatoes, carrots, peas and mash well. Grind ginger and green chilies. Mix it with the chopped coriander leaves, dry fruit, and salt. Take some potato mixture, flatten, place a little stuffing in center and make small balls. Dip the balls in the urad dhal batter and deep fry. Soak the fried vadas in buttermilk for 1/2 hour. Remove, squeeze gently to remove excess liquid and place in a serving dish. Pour beaten yogurt over it. Sprinkle salt, cumin powder, and red chili powder. Serve garnished with chopped coriander.

DHOKLA

1 cup semolina
1 cup yogurt (curd)
1 cup water
1/4 tsp turmeric powder
1 tsp salt

1 1/2 tsp Eno fruit salt
1/4 tsp mustard seeds
2 tsp coriander leaves
  (chopped)
a few curry leaves

Mix semolina, yogurt, water, salt and turmeric powder and keep aside for 2-3 hours to ferment. Mix the Eno fruit salt and pour mixture into a microwave safe dish. Cover with plastic wrap and cook in microwave for approximately 12 mins. Heat oil and add mustard seeds, curry leaves and green chilies. Pour this over the dhokla. Cut into squares, and garnish with coriander leaves.

CORN PATTIES

Potato mixture
450 gms boiled and
  mashed potatoes
2 heaped tbs cornflour
1/2 tsp salt

Filling
250 gms corn kernels
4 cloves crushed garlic
5 green chilies, finely chopped

2 tsp chopped coriander leaves
1/4 tsp turmeric
salt to taste
1 tsp garam masala
2 tsp oil
half a lemon
3/4 tsp coriander and cumin
  powder

oil for frying

Add cornflour and salt to the mashed potatoes. Let it cool. Grate corn kernels. Heat oil, add chilies, garlic, corn, turmeric, salt, coriander and cumin powder and garam masala powder. Cook for a few minutes. Add lemon juice and coriander leaves and let cool. To make patties Take 2 tbs. potato mixture in the palm of your hand, and flatten it. Put 1 tsp corn mixture in center, and cover all sides. Press a little and deep fry until golden brown.

MACARONI AND CHEESE CUTLETS

100 grams macaroni
  (boiled and drained)
2 tsp butter
1 cup all purpose flour
2 cups milk

1 cup grated cheese
1 onion, chopped
salt and pepper to taste
1/2 cup bread crumbs

Melt butter, and lightly saute the onions. Add all purpose flour, little at a time, stirring well. Add milk, constantly stirring till it leaves the sides of the pan, and forms a soft dough. Next add the boiled macaroni, salt, pepper and grated cheese. Mix well. Cool and shape as desired. Roll in bread crumbs and deep fry. Serve hot with tomato sauce.

BREAD AND CHEESE BALLS

9 slices fresh bread (crumbled)
8 tbsp yogurt (curds)
salt to taste
oil for frying

Filling
1 onion chopped
4 tbs. cheese grated
1tbs coriander finely chopped
2 green chilies finely chopped

Mix the bread, yogurt and salt to form a dough. Roll it into balls and set aside. Mix the ingredients for the filling. Flatten each ball and place the filling in it, shape it into balls and deep fry. Serve hot with chutney and tomato sauce.

VEGETABLE CAKE

1/2 kg. or 1 1/4 lbs. potatoes
1/4 kg. or 1/2 lbs. carrots
1/3 kg. or 2 1/4 lbs. peas
200 grams or 1 1/2 cups
  bread crumbs

Green chutney
1 bunch coriander leaves
4 green chilies
4 tsp. sugar
juice of 1/4 lemon
salt to taste

Sweet chutney
100 grams or 4 oz. tamarind
200 grams or 8 oz. dates
100 grams or 8 tbs. sugar
salt to taste
chili powder to taste
2 cups water

Boil potatoes mash and add salt to taste. Boil peas, mash and add salt to taste. Grate carrots, boil and add salt to taste. To make sweet chutney, boil the tamarind, dates, sugar, salt to taste and water to form a thick paste. Cool and strain. To make the green chutney, grind all of the ingredients to a fine paste. Take a round dish and layer 1/3 of the mashed potatoes at the base. Spread green chutney and sweet chutney over the potatoes. Repeat layering with 1/3 of the mashed potatoes, carrots, and mashed peas. Finally, cover with the last 1/3 of the mashed potatoes. Decorate cake with tomato slices, grated carrot, or capsicum, cut into decorative shapes. Bake cake in oven at for 400° 5 min. Serve with both chutneys.

GOLD COIN

1 loaf bread
4 spring onions
1 cup all-purpose flour
1 cup bread crumbs
For Stuffing:
100 grams carrots
2 potatoes
100 grams beans
1 large capsicum
100 grams peas

1 small stalk celery
100 grams cauliflower
100 grams cabbage
100 grams onions
6-8 green Chilies
1/4 inch piece ginger
coriander leaves
salt to taste
oil for frying
1/2 tsp. each of cumin
    and mustard seeds.

Chop and boil all the vegetables except onions, and mash lightly. Heat 1 tbs. of oil. Add cumin and mustard seeds. Add chopped onions and fry for 2-3 minutes. Mix this into the mashed vegetables, and keep aside to cool.

Cut bread slices with a round cookie cutter to make small 2" rounds. Make a thin batter with the all-purpose flour (Maid), salt and 1 cup water. Spread a tbs. of the vegetable mixture on bread rounds, pressing lightly to retain the round shape. Dip them into batter, roll in bread crumbs and deep fry till golden brown. Serve with green chutney or ketchup.

BREAD DAHIWADA

10 Slices Bread
1 cup mint leaves
1 cup coriander leaves
1/2 tsp. tamarind paste
2 tsp fresh coconut, grated
1 cup gram flour (besan)
1 tsp chili powder

1 litre yogurt or curd
1 tsp sugar
1/2 cup chopped coriander
water
salt and sugar to taste

Remove the crust from the bread slices. Grind together, 1 cup mint leaves, 1 cup coriander leaves, tamarind, coconut, salt and sugar with a little water to form a thick chutney. Spread this chutney on one side of bread, cover with another slice. Cut the sandwiched bread into fours. Repeat with the remaining bread. Mix 1 cup gram flour, tsp chili powder and salt to taste with enough water to make a batter. Dip the bread squares into the batter and deep fry till golden brown. Mix the yogurt, salt and sugar and enough water till smooth. Add the fried bread squares to the yogurt, garnish with the 1/2 cup of coriander leaves before serving.

BAMBINO WADA

1/2 kg potatoes
1/4 kg Bambino brand noodles
  (available in Indian
  grocery stores)
6 green chilies
1/2 cup chopped
  coriander leaves

2 onions finely chopped
1 piece ginger, finely chopped
1 cup gram flour (besan)
2 tsp chili powder
salt to taste
oil for frying

Boil and strain the bambino noodles according to directions. Boil and mash the potatoes. Mix all of the ingredients. Shape into small round patties and deep fry in hot oil. Serve with mint chutney.

GOLI BAJE
(A MANGALORE SPECIALTY)

2 cups maida or all purpose flour
2 tbs gram flour (besan)
2 tsp sugar
1/2 cup buttermilk
1 tsp soda bicarbonate
4 green chilies

1" piece ginger, finely chopped
salt to taste
1/3 cup finely chopped coconut
1/2 cup water
oil for deep frying

Mix all ingredients into a thick mixture and keep aside for one hour. Shape into small balls and deep fry till golden brown. Serve with coconut chutney.

METHI KADUBU

2-3 cups fenugreek leaves
   (methi), finely chopped
1 cup Uncle Ben's rice
   (boiled rice)
1 cup long grain rice (raw rice)
2 tsp urad dal (skinless split
   black beans)
1 tsp coriander seeds
1/2 tsp cumin seeds
3-4 dry red chilies
salt to taste

Masala
1/2 cup fresh coconut, grated
1tsp roasted coriander seeds
1/2 tsp cumin seeds, roasted
a pinch of fenugreek
   seeds, roasted
6 dry red chilies, roasted
small lemon sized ball
   of tamarind
1 onion, finely chopped
1 tsp mustard seeds
1 tsp oil
a few curry leaves

Soak together the rice and dal for 2 to 3 hours. Grind coarsely along with coriander seeds, cumin and red chilies. Add the chopped fenugreek leaves and salt. Mix well, pour into greased 'thali' or plate and steam. Cut into squares. Grind all the masala ingredients, i.e., coconut, coriander seeds, cumin seeds, tamarind, fenugreek seeds and red chilies to a fine paste. Heat oil, fry mustard seeds, add chopped onions and curry leaves and fry for 1 minute. Add the masala paste and 3 cups of water and bring to a boil. Add salt to taste. Add the steamed squares and cook for 5 more minutes. Garnish with coriander leaves and serve.

MAIDA CHAKKULI

1 kg all-purpose flour (maida)   100 gms sesame seeds (til)
1/2 cup urad dal (skinless split   salt to taste
  black beans)   oil for frying
1 tsp ghee (clarified butter)

Roast the urad dal till light brown and soak in water for one hour. Tie the all-purpose flour in a muslin cloth and steam for one hour. Remove from cloth and sieve the flour to remove any coarse particles. Grind the soaked dal to a fine paste. Add the flour. Mix well with salt, 1 tsp ghee and sesame seeds. Divide into 2 portions. Add just enough water to one portion at a time to make a soft pliable dough. Put into shakkuli mould, make small rounds with all of the dough. Deep fry till crisp and golden brown. Store in airtight container.

VEGETABLE SPRING ROLLS

1 cup carrots, chopped very fine   *spring roll wrappers*
1 cup beans, chopped very fine   1/4 kg. marida or all purpose
1 cup capsicum, cut into thin   flour
  thin long strips   6 eggs
1/2 cup sprouted moong beans   1 cup milk
1 cup chopped onion   salt and pepper to taste
6-8 cloves of garlic chopped
1" piece ginger grated

Boil all vegetables, keeping them crunchy. Heat 2 tsp. oil and saute the onions. Add ginger and chopped garlic. Add salt, pepper, pinch of ajinonroto (optional), and 1 tsp. of chopped green chilies (optional). Mix and set aside to cool.

To make the wrappers, mix all ingredients into a pouring consistency. Pour a spoonful into a pan till the pan in a circular motion, to form a large thin crepe (about 10" round). Cook only on one side. Turn the cooked side up, place a tablespoon of the vegetable filling down the center. Fold and seal the sides securely with a paste made out of all-purpose flour and a little water. Shallow fry the spring rolls until golden and crisp. Cut into rounds and serve with tomato ketchup.

The spring roll wrappers can also be made by mixing 1/2 kg. all-purpose flour, 1 tsp. oil, salt to taste and enough warm water to form a hard dough. Keep aside for 1/2 hour. Roll into thin round chapatis and cook only on one side. Then proceed to make the spring rolls as above.

MOONG DAL WADA

2 cups moong dal (split green moong beans)
10 green chilies
1/2" piece ginger
1 cup coriander leaves, chopped

1 large onion, chopped fine
2-3 slices of bread
salt to taste
oil for frying

Soak moong dal for 1 hour. Strain out the water and grind it together with the green chilies, ginger, and salt without adding water. Finally add the onions, coriander leaves and the bread (softened by soaking in warm water and then squeezing out all excess liquid). Grind everything for 1 minute till it is mixed well. Make small balls, press lightly to flatten and deep fry. Serve with coriander chutney.

POHA WADA

2 cups beaten rice (poha)
2-3 potatoes boiled and mashed.
1 cup gram flour (besan)
5 green chilies
1/2 cup coriander leaves
a few curry leaves, chopped

1 tsp. red chili powder
1/4 tsp. hing
1" piece ginger
salt to taste
oil for frying

Wash the beaten rice, add to the mashed potatoes, Mix well adding the rest of the ingredients. Shape into small balls, press lightly to flatten and deep fry till crisp and golden brown. Serve with ketchup or coriander chutney.

CABBAGE BONDA

1/4 kg. cabbage, chopped fine
1 onion, chopped fine
5 green chilies, chopped
1 tsp. coriander leaves, chopped

1 1/2" piece ginger
1 cup gram flour (besan)
salt to taste
oil for frying

Mix all ingredients lightly, carefully adding just enough water to form a thick mixture. Shape into round balls and deep fry in oil till brown.

POTATO RAVA WADA

1/2 kg. potatoes
  (boiled and mashed)
1/4 kg. semolina (bombay rava)
1/2 cup yogurt or curd
1" piece ginger, chopped fine

2 tbs. coriander leaves,
  chopped fine
2 sprigs of curry leaves,
  chopped
salt to taste
oil for frying

Mix all ingredients without adding any water. Shape into round balls and deep fry in oil till golden brown.

BREAD BONDA

6 slices of bread
1 cup mixed vegetables
1 onion, chopped
3-4 green chilies

1" piece ginger
2 tbs. coriander, chopped
salt to taste
oil for frying

To make the filling, heat 1 tbs. oil and saute the onions, green chilies and ginger. Add the mixed vegetables, coriander leaves and salt to taste. Cook till done.

Remove the crusts of the bread slices and soak them in water. Remove immediately, placing them between the palms of your hands, squeeze out all excess liquid. Repeat with the remaining bread. Place a tbs. of the vegetable filling down the center of the bread, fold and press firmly to seal all edges. Deep fry in hot oil till golden brown.

BALEKAYI CUTLET

2 raw bananas (plantains)
  boiled
2 potatoes, boiled
3 green chilies, chopped
4 cloves garlic
1/2" piece of ginger
1/2 cup chopped
  coriander leaves

2 slices of bread
2 onions chopped fine
1 tsp. oil
1/2 tsp. garam masla
salt to taste
oil for shallow frying

Peel and mash the boiled potatoes and raw banana. Heat 1 tsp. oil and fry the onions, garlic, ginger, chilies, coriander leaves and salt to taste. Soak the bread in water, remove and squeeze out excess liquid. Mix all of the above very well, shape into round or oval flat cutlets. Roll in bread crumbs or rice flour and shallow fry till golden brown.

PAPER KEBAB

250 gms. ground or minced
  chicken
5 gms. ginger paste
5 gms. garlic paste
50 gms. onions chopped

10 gms. grated cheese
2 eggs
salt to taste
aluminum foil

Mix together ground chicken, ginger, garlic, onions, cheese, eggs and salt to taste. Shape into small sausages. Cut square pieces of aluminum foil. Place kebab in center, roll and crimp edges well to seal. Deep fry in hot oil. When they begin to float on the surface, kebabs are done. Remove and serve with mint chutney.

AFGHANI KEBAB

4 boneless chicken breast pieces
10 gms. garlic
10 gms. ginger
10 gms. green chilies
10 gms. coriander leaves

50 gms. cream
10 gms. grated cheese
200 gms. minced or
  ground chicken
salt and pepper to taste

Mix together ground chicken, chopped ginger, garlic, chilies, coriander leaves and salt. Heat a tbs. of oil in a pan and fry this mixture till half cooked. Set aside to cool. Using a sharp knife, slice horizontally along the middle of the chicken breast. Place the ground chicken mixture inside each chicken breast. Apply the cream and cheese all over, place in a shallow baking dish, drizzle with 1 tbs. oil and bake in a moderately hot oven till done. Towards the end, raise the temperature to broil until the surface is brown and grilled. Serve with mint chutney.

BREAD BASUNDI

2 liters milk
6 slices of bread
1 tin condense milk

5 tbs. sugar
a little saffron (kesar)

Remove crust and break up bread into small pieces. Add it to the milk along with saffron and boil the milk till it is reduced to half the quantity. Add the condensed milk and sugar. Let it cool. You may garnish with some roasted chironjc seeds and serve.

NENDRA BANANA HALWA

9 nendra bananas
1 cup sugar
1 cup ghee (clarified butter)

7 cardamoms, powdered
banana essence (optional)

Add sugar to 1/3 cup water to make a syrup. Cut bananas into small pieces and add to the boiling syrup. When bananas are soft and well cooked, add the ghee a little at a time, stirring constantly. Add cardamom powder and banana essence to give it added flavor. When mixture turns dark brown and the ghee separates from it, the halwa is done. Spread on a platter. Cool and cut into pieces.

DUDHI HALWA

1 kg. dudhi (bottle gord)
400 gms. mava (dried
  whole milk)

350 gms. sugar
1/2 tsp. rose water
silver foil for decorating

Peel and grate the dudhi. Boil in water and strain. Add sugar to the dudhi and cook in a heavy bottom pan till it is almost dry. Crumble the mava and add to the cooked dudhi. Add rose water. Spread on a thali or platter, decorate with silver foil.

KAR KUMBADA HALWA

1 kg. white pumpkin
  (remove peel and seeds)
1 cup cream

2 cups sugar
1/2 cup ghee (clarified butter)
chopped nuts for garnish

Grate and cook the pumpkin in it's own juice till dry. Add cream and sugar. Continue stirring till completely dry and brown in color. Add ghee and cook till ghee floats to the top. Remove, decorate with chopped nuts and serve.

ELAPPA

1/4 cup moong dal
  (split green moong beans)
1/2 cup urad dal
  (skinless black beans)
1/2 kg. long grained rice
1 tsp. methi seeds (fenugreek)
1/2 fresh coconut, grated

3 ripe bananas
1/2 cup beaten rice
1 cup half cooked rice
1/2 kg. jaggery
pinch of salt
3 tsp. sesame seeds
oil for frying

Soak both dals in water for 1 hour. Grind together with the rest of the ingredients adding very little water to make a thick batter. Heat oil, take spoonfuls of batter and deep fry till golden brown.

MALPURI

1 cup maida (all purpose flour)
2 tsp. fine rava (semolina)
3/4 cup sugar

a little saffron
ghee for frying

Mix maida with 3/4 cup of water. Add rava saffron and sugar and keep aside for 15-20 minutes. Heat some ghee in a small frying pan. Pour a large spoonful of batter, fry on both sides until crisp and brown. Repeat with the rest of the batter.

SEVEN CUPS SWEET

1 cup besan (chick pea flour)
1 cup maida (all purpose flour)
1 cup milk
1 cup dry coconut powder
2 cups sugar

3/4 cup ghee (clarified butter)
1/2 tsp. cardamom powder
chopped cashew nuts for
 garnish

Mix all the ingredients and cook on a slow fire, stirring constantly.
When the mixture starts to leave the sides, pour into a greased
platter and cut into squares while still hot. Garnish with
cashew nuts.

ATHIRASE

2 cups rice
2 cups jaggery
2 tsp. khus-khus (poppy seeds)

1 ripe banana
oil for frying

Soak the rice for 3 days, changing the water every day. Strain
well and spread to dry. When dry, powder the rice and pass it
through a sieve. Add softened jaggery and mashed banana to
the rice flour and pound well to mix. Form small balls, flatten
to shape like large cookies. Sprinkle and press into surface
the poppy seeds. Deep fry in hot oil till golden brown and
remove.

SHRIKHAND

8 cups thick yogurt or curds
4 cups sugar
1 tsp. cardamom powder
2 tsp. chopped almonds
 and pistachios

1 tsp. chivonji nuts
1/2 tsp. saffron soaked in
 a tbs. of milk

SHRIKHAND (continued)

Pour the yogurt into a muslin or a cheesecloth, tie the ends and suspend it for 4-5 hours until all liquid has been completely strained. Remove, add sugar, cardamom powder and the saffron. Beat well to form a smooth paste. Serve garnished with the chopped almonds, pistachios and chironji nuts.

Cakes and Biscuits

CARROT CAKE

1 cup margarine or refined oil
3/4 cup sugar
4 small eggs
2 cups plain flour
2 tsp. baking powder
1 cup chopped almonds
2 cups grated carrots
a pinch of salt

Icing
225 gms. cream cheese
1 cup icing sugar

Mix margarine and sugar together. Add eggs and mix well. Fold in the flour, baking powder and salt. Lastly add the carrots and nuts. Mix well and pour into greased pan and bake at 350°F for 45 minutes. Blend together cream cheese and icing sugar. Slice the cooled cake horizontally into half. Spread the icing in between, and all over cake.

EGG-LESS CAKE

1/2 can condensed milk
125 gms. All purpose flour
1 tsp. baking powder
1/2 tsp. soda bicarbonate
50 gms. butter

50 gms powdered sugar
1/2 tsp. vanilla essence
1 cup milk
yellow food coloring
 (optional)

Melt the butter till soft. Add sugar, condensed milk, food coloring and vanilla essence. Beat well for 15 minutes. Fold in the sieved all purpose flour with baking powder and and soda bicarbonate. Add milk and mix. Pour into greased and floured pan and bake in a 350°F oven for 20-30 minutes.

BANANA CAKE

2 cups all purpose flour
1/2 cup sugar
1/2 cup chopped nuts
1/2 cup butter
1/2 cup buttermilk
2 ripe bananas

2 eggs
1/2 tsp. baking powder
1/2 tsp. salt
1 tsp. vanilla essence
1/2 tsp. baking soda

Heat oven to 350°F. Combine all ingredients except the flour and nuts. Mix at low speed until moistened. Mix at medium speed for 3 minutes. Fold in the flour and nuts. Mix and pour into a greased and floured cake pan, and bake for approximately 35 minutes.

BLACK FOREST CAKE

6 eggs
1 cup powdered sugar
1/2 cup flour
1/3 cup cocoa powder
1/2 cup butter
1/2 tsp. salt
1 tsp. vanilla essence
1 tsp. baking powder

Syrup
1/3 cup sugar
3 tsp. water
2 tsp. rum

1/3 cup cherries
1/2 cup sweetened
whipped cream

Beat the eggs with powdered sugar till light and fluffy. Sift flour with cocoa powder, baking powder and salt. Melt butter and cool a little. Fold in the flour and butter into the eggs. Add the vanilla essence and mix well. Pour batter into two greased and floured pans and bake at 350°F for approximately 20 minutes. To make the syrup, boil the sugar with water for 1 min. and cool. Add 2 tsp. rum and drizzle syrup over the cakes. Sandwich the cakes with the whipped cream and decorate the top with remaining cream and cherries.

COCONUT CAKE

3 eggs
1/2 cup butter
1/2 cup fresh cream
3/4 cup sugar
1 cup all purpose flour

1/2 tsp. vanilla essence
1/2 cup dry coconut flakes
1/2 tsp. baking powder
a pinch of salt

Sift the flour with baking powder. Beat the butter and sugar together. Add eggs, vanilla essence and beat again. Fold in the cream and coconut and mix well. Pour in a greased cake pan and cook in a 350°F oven till done.

NO-BAKE CHOCOLATE CAKE

200 gms. Marie biscuits
  or tea biscuits (crumbled)
2 tbs. chopped walnuts
40 gms. Chocolate(cut in pieces)

2 tbs. chopped raisins
100 gms. butter
75 gms. honey
50 gms. Cocoa powder
  (sieved)

Mix biscuit crumbs, walnuts, raisins and chocolate pieces together. Beat the butter and sugar until light and fluffy. Add honey and beat again. Fold in the cocoa powder and biscuit crumbs and mix well. Spoon mixture into a baking pan, cover and freeze till set. Remove. Slice and serve.

EASY BISCUITS

200 gms. flour
200 gms. powdered sugar
150 gms. shortening

a few cashewnuts
1 tsp. cardamom powder
1 tsp. semolina (fine) or sooji

Mix sugar, flour and semolina in a bowl. Melt shortening and pour into the flour. Mix to form a soft dough. Make small balls, place on a greased cookie tray, and bake in a 350°F oven for 30 minutes.

COCONUT COOKIES

1/2 cup dry coconut flakes
1 cup all purpose flour
1/2 cup sugar
1/2 cup clarified butter (ghee)
1/2 tsp. vanilla essence

4 tsp. coconut milk or
  plain milk
4 tsp. baking powder
4 tsp. milk
1/2 tsp. cardamom powder

Mix all the ingredients, except coconut, adding a little milk if it is dry. Keep aside for 5 minutes. Roll on a floured cutting board till 1/4 inch thick. Sprinkle milk and the dry coconut over the dough. Cut into desired shape. Place on a greased tray and bake at 350°F for 30 minutes.

MELTING MOMENTS

100 gms. butter
75 gms. powdered sugar
125 gms. all purpose flour
1/4 tsp. baking powder

50 gms. corn flakes
A few dried cherries
1/2 tsp. vanilla essence
1 egg

Beat sugar, butter, and egg. Add flour, baking powder, and vanilla essence and mix. Make balls and roll into crushed corn flakes. Press half a cherry into the center of the ball. Place on greased tray and bake at 350°F for 15 minutes.

CHILI BISCUITS

150 gms. all purpose flour
75 gms. butter or shortening
10 gms. sugar
3/4 tsp. baking powder

10 gms. green chilies
10 gms. curry leaves
10 gms. coriander leaves
3 tsp. yogurt

Mix all of the ingredients to form a soft dough. Roll out on a floured board and cut into desired shape. Bake at 350°F for 15 minutes.

SEMOLINA (SOOJI) BISCUITS

1/3 cup fine semolina
225 gms. all purpose flour
170 gms. sugar
1 large egg

1/2 tsp. baking powder
150 gms. butter
a few drops of vanilla essence
a pinch of salt

Cream butter and sugar. Add rest of the ingredients. Roll on a floured board and cut into desired shapes. Bake at 350°F for 15 minutes.

Desserts

LEMON PIE

1 can condensed milk
2 eggs, whites and yolks
   separated
1/2 tsp. lime juice

10-12 marie biscuits or tea
   biscuits
1 tsp. butter
2 tbs. powdered sugar

Powder biscuits very fine and mix it with the melted butter.
Press this mixture firmly into the base and sides of a pie dish.
Whisk together condensed milk, egg yolks, lime juice and
sugar. Pour into the prepared pie dish. Beat the egg whites and
powdered sugar separately, till it form stiff peaks. Pour into pie
dish and bake in a 350°F oven for about 20 mins., or till the top
of the pie starts to turn a golden brown.

PINEAPPLE CHEESE CAKE

500 gms. paneer
300 gms. fresh cream
1 tin condensed milk
2 cups custard without sugar
(made with 2 1/2 cups milk
   and 2 tbs. custard powder)
1 1/2 tbs. gelatin

1 small tin pineapple pieces
a few slices of pineapple
crust:
15 marie biscuits or tea
   biscuits
2 tbs. melted butter

Powder the biscuits very finely. Mix it with the melted butter
and press mixture into bottom and sides of a shallow dish. Chill.
Mix the paneer and custard and blend well. Add condensed
milk, cream dissolved gelatin and beat till creamy. Blend the
pineapple pieces in its own juice and add it to the above mixture.
Pour mixture into the chilled dish. Decorate with pineapple
slices. Keep in freezer until set, later transfer to refrigerator.

CHARLOTTE RUSSE

1 tin condensed milk
1 tin evaporated or thick milk
plain yogurt measured in the same tin

Mix all the ingredients, pour into a pan and steam for 20 minutes. Cool and invert onto a plate and garnish with chocolate curls.

LEMON DELIGHT

2 eggs
1 cup milk
1 tbs. flour
1 tbs. butter

5 tbs. sugar
1 cup milk
juice of 1 lemon

Cream egg yolks and sugar until light and fluffy. Add the butter and flour gradually and beat till foamy. Add milk and lemon juice mix. Fold in the beaten egg whites. Pour into a greased baking dish and bake till the top turns golden brown. Serve either hot or cold.

ZUNNU

6 eggs
1 cup condensed milk
1 cup carnation milk or milk powder

Blend the ingredients and pour into a buttered pan. Bake for 45-60 minutes in a 350°F oven.

QUICK LEMON SOUFFLE

1 family size pack vanilla ice-cream
2 pkts. lemon jelly crystals (jello)
2 bananas sliced

Dissolve jelly crystals in 4 cups of water and cool. Refrigerate till half set. Mix together vanilla ice-cream and half of the jelly with a beater. Pour into a mould and set in refrigerator. Decorate with banana slices and remaining jelly and serve.

SNOWFLAKE PUDDING

2 cups milk
1 cup sugar
1 cup heavy cream
1/2 cup grated coconut (fresh)
1 tsp. vanilla essence
1 tbs. gelatin

Dissolve the gelatin in 4 tbs. hot water. Boil the milk and add sugar and dissolved gelatin and cool. Add heavy cream, grated coconut and mix well. Pour into a dish and set in refrigerator.

APPLE CHEESE CAKE

2 eggs
1/4 cup powdered sugar
1/2 tbs. lemon juice
1/2 tsp. lemon rind
3 tsp. gelatin
1 cup apple, pieces cut
  to desired shapes.
1 1/2 cups pureed apples
180 gms. marie biscuits
  (graham crackers)
40 gms. butter
1/2 cup milk 100 gms.
  paneer (cottage cheese)

Mix crumbled biscuits and butter and roast lightly until you get a good aroma. Line a dish with this mixture and set in freezer. Beat the yolks, powdered sugar, lemon juice and rind. Cook in a double boiler until it thickens. Add dissolved gelatin, mix and let it cool. Grate paneer and blend into above mixture along with apple puree and milk. Finally fold in the beaten egg whites. Pour into a dish and garnish with apple pieces. Chill in refrigerator till set.

MOCHA CHOCOLATE SOUFFLE

1 cup milk
1 tbs. custard powder
45 gms. drinking chocolate
1 cup condensed milk

10 gms. sugar
20 gms. gelatin
a few chopped nuts for
 garnish

Make custard with custard powder, milk and drinking chocolate (stir while cooling so that no cream is formed). When cool, add dissolved gelatin and condensed milk. Beat for a few minutes and pour into a wet mould. Keep in refrigerator to set. Unmould onto a plate. Decorate with nuts before serving.

MANGO DELIGHT

2 eggs
100 gms. paneer
500 gms. milk
500 gms. mango pulp
150 gms. sugar

1 cup cream
15 gms. gelatin
colored wafer biscuits
chopped nuts for garnishing

Separate yolks from whites, beat the yolks with sugar. Add the boiled milk and make a thick custard. Let it cool, then add dissolved gelatin, whipped cream and mango pulp. Gradually fold in beaten egg whites. Pour into a glass dish and let it set in the refrigerator. Garnish with wafers and nuts and serve chilled.

FUN WITH MOULD

1 pkt. lemon jelly crystals
(jello)

2 oranges

1 tin pineapple slices

3 tbs. powdered sugar

6 tbs. sugar

1 pkt. marie biscuits
(graham crackers)

1/2 tbs. pineapple or vanilla
essence

1 1/2 cups fresh cream

1 1/2 cup milk

1/2 cup glazed cherries

1 cup walnuts

2 tbs. custard powder
(vanilla flavor)

Dissolve jelly crystals in two cups of hot water. Take 4 or 5 pineapple slices. Dip them in the jelly syrup and layer them on the base of the mould. Pour half of the jelly syrup on this and leave to set in refrigerator. Make thick custard with the custard powder and milk and let it cool. To this add heavy cream, essence and powdered sugar and beat well. Pour this into the refrigerated mould and layer the remaining jelly over this. Sprinkle the powdered marie biscuits over this and let it set in the refrigerator. Just before serving, dip the mould in warm water. Turn it over onto a plate and decorate it with orange and pineapple slices, glazed cherries and walnuts.

FLUFFY LEMON TRIFLE

1 kg. Sponge cake

1 cup sugar

syrup (1/2 cup sugar dissolved
in 1/2 cup water)

3 eggs separated

1 tin condensed milk

3 lemons

50 gms. almonds (blanched,
sliced, and toasted) for
topping

Crumble the sponge cake and layer the bowl with it. Sprinkle the sugar syrup over this, just enough to soak the crumbs. Cook the egg yolks, condensed milk, lemon juice and rind over low heat till it thickens. Let it cool. Beat the egg whites until stiff and blend into the custard. Pour this into the bowl to cover the layer of sponge cake. Let it set in the refrigerator. Decorate with whipped cream and almonds before serving.

NUTTY COFFEE SOUFFLÉ

3 tsp. instant coffee powder
2 tsp. gelatin
3 eggs
150 gms sugar (powdered)

1 cup cream
1 1/2 cups hot water
2 tbs. crushed walnuts

Dissolve gelatin in 1/2 cup hot water. Mix coffee powder in 1 cup of hot water. Beat egg yolks with powdered sugar till creamy. Add dissolved coffee and gelatin and beat for 1 minute. Add cream and beat for 2 minutes. Beat egg whites separately till stiff peaks are formed. Gently fold in egg whites into remainder of mixture. Pour into bowl, decorate with crushed walnuts, cover and leave in freezer till it sets. Immediately transfer to refrigerator.

APRICOTS AND ICE-CREAM

50 gms. butter
200 gms. tea biscuits or
  graham crackers
500 gms. dried apricots
  (soaked overnight in
  1 cup water)

3/4 cup sugar
 ice cream
1 large carton vanilla
2 tbs. gelatin
1 cup heavy cream

Crumble graham crackers, mix with melted butter and press mixture into sides and bottom of a pie dish. Bake in a moderately hot oven for 5 minuttes. Boil apricots with sugar. Remove seeds and lightly puree. Blend pureed apricots with dissolved gelatin. Gradually add ice cream and heavy cream blending gently. Pour into prepared dish and refrigerate till it sets.

FRUIT SALAD CHEESCAKE

10 marie tea biscuits or
  graham crackers
2 tbs. crushed nuts
  (cashewnuts and walnuts)
2 tbs. milk powder
2 tsp. cinnamon powder
2 tsp. butter, melted

For topping:
3/4 cup yogurt
1/2 cup sugar
1 pack lemon jelly crystals or
  jello (prepared as per
  directions)
1 8 oz. package cream cheese
  (or paneer made with
  1 litre of milk)
1 30 oz. can preserved fruit
  cocktail
1 tsp. lemon rind
1 tsp. vanilla essence
1 cup heavy cream

Crush biscuits, and mix well together with milk powder, cinnamon, butter and crushed nuts. Press mixture firmly into bottom and sides of pie dish and refrigerate. When half set, remove and add the cream and fruit cocktail. Mix and pour into the prepared dish. Garnish with lemon rind and chill to set.

BREAD PUDDING

6 slices of bread
4 eggs
1/4 cup butter
1/4 cup sugar
1/2 tsp. vanilla essense

1/4 tsp. nutmeg powder
2 cups warm milk
1/2 cup pineapple jam
2 tbs. sugar

Remove crust from bread slices. Butter bread and set aside. Mix well, 2 whole eggs, 2 egg yolks, 1/4 cup sugar, nutmeg powder and vanilla essence. Place bread slices in glass dish and pour egg mixture over it. Bake at 350°F, till the mixture becomes firm (approximately 1/2 hour). Remove and apply a layer of jam. Place back into oven, untill egg whites start to turn golden brown.

TENDER COCONUT SOUFFLÉ

1 tin condensed milk
2 tins tender coconut water
4 tins milk
3 tbs. gelatin

1 cup tender coconut, cut
 into strips
1 tsp. vanilla essense

Soak gelatin in 2 cups of tender coconut water for 5 minutes. Heat and stir till dissolved. Mix all of the ingredients. Pour into a dish and freeze till it sets. Immediately transfer to refrigerator.

❧ NOTES ❧

.

Ingredients

DRY MEASUREMENT:
0.035 ounces...................1 gram
1 ounce...........................26.35 gram
1 pound...........................453.59 grams/0.45kg
2.21 pounds......................1 kilogram

LIQUID MEASUREMENT:
1 teaspoon...........................4.9ml
1 tablespoon..........................14.8 ml
1/2 cup..................................237 ml
1 cup.....................................237 ml
1.06 quarts.............................1000ml/1liter

Detroit, MI
India Grocers Inc.,
34714 Dequindre Road
Sterling Heights, MI, 48310
Ph: (810) 795-0012

Portland, OR
India Direct Inc.,
16205 SW Bethany, OR 97006
Ph: (503) 690-0499
or 1-888-99-INDIA

San Jose, CA
Sushma Emporium
480-A Blossom Hill Road
San Jose, CA
Ph: (408) 281-0392

Chicago, IL
Indian Groceries & Spices
7300 St., Louis Avenue
Skokie, IL
Ph: (847) 674-2480

Milwaukee, WI
Indian Groceries & Spices Intl.,
10633 W. North Avenue
Milwaukee, WI
Ph: (414) 771-3535

Harrisburg, PA
India Groceries and Fashions
2650 Walnut Street
Harrisburg, PA
Ph: (717) 236-7345

Long Island, NY
King of Spices
3336 Hillside Avenue
New Hyde Park, NY 11040
Ph: (516) 739-5464

Pittsburgh, PA
Patel Brothers
3821 William Penn Highway
Monroeville, PA 15146
Ph: (412) 372-2758

Pittsburgh, PA
Indian Groceries
5040 William Penn Highway
Murrysville, PA 15668
Ph: (724) 325-3665

Pittsburgh, PA
Indian Groceries
3936 Monroeville Blvd.
Monroeville, PA 15146
Ph: (724) 325-3665

Pittsburgh, PA
Bombay Emporium
294 Craft Avenue
Pittsburgh, PA 15213
Ph: (412) 682-4965

Printed in Great Britain
by Amazon